EMPOWERED
&
AWAKENED

A Guide to Breakthrough Self-Doubt,
Reclaim Your Self-Worth,
and Unlock the Divine Vision for Your Life

MARIAH GISCOMBE

Dedication

This book is dedicated with my greatest love to my amazing daughter Jahniah (a.k.a my ace, my heart, my 2.0 and my birthday twin), who brings so much love, light, and laughter into my life.

Table of Contents

Introduction

Have you ever reached rock bottom in your life? The season where you felt like your life was progressively spiraling downward but you couldn't hit the emergency brake? There is nothing pretty about feeling so out of control of your own life that you don't even know where to start picking up the pieces.

When your life falls apart, it is a surreal experience. It is as though you have come out of your body and are witnessing the chaos taking place as an observer, looking in. You watch as each aspect of your life—your relationships, career, finances, and health—starts crumbling down right before your eyes. Of course, you want to act with immediate effect, but how useful is your action when you have mentally dissociated from your reality, terrified of confronting the present moment and bringing an end to the destruction?

When my life fell apart, just before my 35th birthday, it seemed unlikely that it would ever be restored. The accumulation of hurt, trauma, and self-limiting beliefs over the decades had caught up with me and demanded to be felt, acknowledged, and released. The pain I felt during that season of my life was a sign that I needed to heal my mind, body, and soul.

In other words, my rock bottom was my catalyst for change. It was the transitional period I needed to heal from my past, let go of destructive habits, break free from dependency on others, and move toward a new stage of life that honored who I truly was and my

God-given destiny. It might sound ironic to say that the lowest point in my life was, in fact, the most significant point of my life because it helped me shed old skin and embrace an empowered and awakened version of myself.

If you were at a crossroads and you could choose to close a painful chapter from your past, would you choose to let it go? As difficult as that choice would be, I believe you would! Who wouldn't want to experience personal breakthroughs, make peace with their past, and increase their sense of self-worth?

I have been coaching for over 10 years, first as a business strategist and now as a certified NLP life and success coach. When I am invited to speaking engagements or see clients on a one-on-one basis, I get asked the same question: *How can I get to the next level of my life?* The answer to that question cannot be summarized in a sentence, so I decided to write this book. Being a healthier and happier version of ourselves has always been a topic on our lips since the time of our ancestors when health meant staying alive. In modern days, being healthy and happy in life can mean gaining self-confidence, cultivating healthy relationships, healing from past traumas, accomplishing career goals, or simply becoming better versions of ourselves.

You might be a working mom or entrepreneur who's used to taking care of others, but make little time to take care of yourself. After surviving a rocky childhood or suppressing years of trauma, the need for a shift in how you live, work, and relate to others has made you ready to undergo a personal transformation. You are ready to dream again and create a fresh vision for your personal and professional life. After taking the more traditional route in life:

graduating from university, getting a stable job, and raising kids, you have realized that there is more life you are yet to experience.

Your ambition, willingness, and calling to break free from your comfort zone make you the perfect candidate for a fresh start! You have the necessary ingredients to thrive in your personal and professional endeavors, but you are still missing the recipe.

Empowered & Awakened is a book about rewriting your life story, reconnecting to your divine self, and living a purpose-driven life. In this book, you will learn tools and strategies which will help you kickstart your awakening (personal transformation). Living a healed and empowered life requires five commitments that make up my signature framework:

1. Identify and transform self-doubt.
2. Prioritize your self-care.
3. Develop self-awareness.
4. Connect to your inner wisdom.
5. Unlock the vision for your life.

Together, we will discuss these various commitments and how they can help you create the life you envision. While transformation doesn't occur overnight, honoring these five commitments will bring noticeable improvements in how you perceive yourself and your ability to succeed at anything you do.

Everything changed when I chose to put the needs of my future self first. I invite you to surrender to your transformational journey and manifest the life of your dreams!

COMMITMENT #1:

Identify and Transform Self-Doubt

CHAPTER 1:

Identifying Your Hidden Saboteurs

The most common way people give up their power is by thinking they don't have any.

— Alice Walker

B e honest with yourself, how many times have you pulled the brakes on your own plans or retreated in fear when you were presented with an opportunity for change? How many people have you rejected because being around them triggered your own insecurities? Or how many times have you discarded advice the moment you felt challenged to confront your norms and beliefs?

I'm sure you have heard the saying, "You are your own worst enemy." Have you ever unpacked it to understand what it means? According to the Cambridge Dictionary, an enemy is "a person who hates or opposes another person and tries to harm them or stop them from doing something" (Cambridge Dictionary, 2019). Thinking of yourself being your own worst enemy sounds pretty harsh, doesn't it? But in reality, when you deny yourself new possibilities or reinforce self-limiting beliefs, you are causing harm to yourself.

If you found out that a close friend of yours was secretly spreading lies about you behind your back, you would probably distance yourself from them. However, what would you do if you realized that your own self-doubt or low self-esteem were stopping you from reaching the next level in your life? Dealing with external enemies is a lot simpler than having to confront yourself. After all, your ego tries, by all means, to defend you, even when you are clearly misguided.

How you think and feel about yourself is far more important than what others think and feel about you. It's time to confront your self-sabotaging behaviors, tune out the voice of the inner critic, and get real about what your beliefs are costing you.

Limiting Beliefs That Stunt Your Growth

How often do you say, "I'm not ready," "I can't," "I will never do that," or "I don't have enough money/experience/time?" Without you even knowing it, your words create limitations in your life that make growth or success seem hard to come by. For example, if you tell yourself that the reason for not starting your business is because you don't have money, how far do you think you will get in manifesting your goal?

Limiting beliefs are the mental barriers that stand in the way of you succeeding in life. They remind you of what you can't do and impose superficial blocks, keeping you stuck in your comfort zone. Limiting beliefs begin as negative ideas or assumptions that you have about your life. When these assumptions are directed at yourself, they end up becoming self-limiting beliefs. In most cases, when you get through a difficult time in life without getting closure or taking the time to heal from the emotional wound caused, you carry a bitter story about what happened and how you can prevent it from happening again.

If you browse through social media, you might come across photos highlighting societal beauty, career, and lifestyle standards. Looking at those photos could make you turn around and question whether you are working hard enough in your life. The thought of not being rich, attractive, or successful enough may cross your mind.

Eventually, limiting beliefs like these can also lead to a low sense of self-worth. Think about it: If you were constantly reminded of your limitations, how would that make you feel? Would you be able to walk into a boardroom and own a meeting? Set up a meeting with your boss and ask for the raise you know you deserve? Or finally, get to sitting down and drawing up your business plan? Having a low sense of self-worth causes you to lose awareness of what you bring to the table. You may feel like you don't fit into certain social spaces or that you don't qualify for certain opportunities.

Your beliefs form how you see yourself in relation to others and the world at large. Having limiting beliefs could lead to feelings of inferiority or setting extremely low expectations for yourself. You may even view others as being comparatively better than you, which can make you value others more than you value yourself. Moreover, when you carry self-limiting beliefs, you find it difficult to follow through with your goals because, at the core of who you are, you don't believe you deserve to live a certain way or enjoy certain experiences. If you are wondering whether you struggle with a low sense of self-worth, here are some common signs to look out for:

- **You set a limitation on how much money you are able to earn.** Income choking occurs when you believe you are not capable of achieving a level of financial freedom. You cap your earnings at a certain income bracket and fear or doubt your ability to generate more money. Common negative money beliefs are: "Money corrupts people," "I don't make enough to invest money," "Wealth is for the upper class only."

- **You react to circumstances whenever you feel triggered.** When you carry doubts about your potential, you tend to think that others lack faith in you too. In essence, you think that people view you as harshly as you view yourself. This causes you to react defensively whenever you perceive others are hinting at your insecurities or exposing your weaknesses.

- **You keep on delaying getting started on your plans.** When you don't see value in who you are, you are constantly afraid of failing, being rejected, or humiliating yourself. Since you don't back yourself, taking on new opportunities seems like a dangerous thing to do. Thus, you can procrastinate getting started on your plans, or make excuses for why you were unable to complete a goal.

- **You are uncomfortable expressing your light.** Every human being is born for a specific purpose. None of us are here to stand on the sidelines and cheer others on. Carrying limiting beliefs can cause you to feel uncomfortable expressing your individuality and natural talents and gifts. Since limiting beliefs distort how you view yourself, they can make you resent your uniqueness, or light, or feel insecure about it. Ironically, you may celebrate the light you see in others and encourage them to continue developing their talents and gifts.

- **You are plagued with fear and insecurity.** There are two motivations in life that guide our decision-making. We are either motivated by love or fear. When we are motivated by love, we are more likely to have empowering beliefs about ourselves and others and see the world as an abundant place. However, when we are motivated by fear, we tend to adopt limiting beliefs that keep us in bondage to our past or comfort zone. When you have a low sense of self-worth you inflate your fears and insecurities more than you embody love.

- **You prioritize the agendas of others above your own.** When you don't see value in yourself, you might think that everyone is better and more deserving than you. This is another example of a distorted perception. You become dependent on external validation since you find value in being affirmed by people who you deem as superior to yourself. This leads to self-sabotaging behaviors like people-pleasing, which dishonor who you are.

Without working through your limiting beliefs, it will be difficult to improve your sense of self-worth. You must first change what you think about yourself in order to change how you see yourself.

Speaking Against Your Breakthrough

Learning how to build healthy romantic relationships has been a recurring theme in my life. While I have never had any problems attracting men, most of the men I would attract in the past were emotionally unavailable. Spending time reflecting on my dating life has helped me make sense of my dating experiences, and figure out what needed to be resolved. In one of my journal entries, I wrote:

Since I started dating, I have never managed to find a good man. I didn't have solid boundaries back then and I certainly don't have solid boundaries now. I feel like I'm destined to attract narcissistic men.

Reading back what I wrote about my dating life told me everything I needed to know about why I had struggled to cultivate healthy romantic relationships. I was carrying unconscious negative beliefs about love, like believing I was unable to attract true love. These unconscious beliefs were sabotaging my efforts to attract the right kind of men.

Let's strip apart how I wrote about my dating life to identify negative beliefs:

1. "I have never managed to find a good man."

While it may be true that I have battled to maintain healthy romantic relationships in the past, saying that I never found a good man before meant that it was impossible for me to suddenly find one now. After all, if you have never succeeded at something, what are the chances of you making a breakthrough now? Instead of damning my past (and subsequently damning my future) by using an exaggeration like "never," I could have rather said, "I haven't found a good man yet." The keyword here would be "yet," which signifies that it is possible for me to make a breakthrough in the future.

2. **"I didn't have solid boundaries back then and I certainly don't have solid boundaries now."**

Okay, I was being honest when I said that I didn't have solid boundaries in the past. However, by linking past behavior with present behavior, I was unconsciously holding myself stuck to old patterns of behavior. Just because I couldn't do something in the past, doesn't mean I still can't do it now. Although part of one story, my past and present are not linked. In other words, my past failures, habits, or traumatic experiences don't have any influence on my capacity to succeed in the present moment. The better way for me to phrase that sentence would have been to say, "I didn't have solid boundaries back then; however, I am confident in my ability to develop solid boundaries now."

3. **"I feel like I'm destined to attract narcissistic men."**

Words carry an immense amount of power. It may seem harmless to combine a few letters and create a word or phrase, but your subconscious mind—the part of your mind that stores your beliefs, habits, and memories—collects every word spoken and stores it as information about your current reality. When you speak poorly about yourself, you develop self-limiting beliefs, which are negative perceptions you hold about yourself that form how you live your life.

When I mentioned being destined to attract low-value men, I was reinforcing a self-limiting belief about my self-worth. Saying I would always attract low-value men meant that I didn't believe I deserved a high-value man or the opportunity of experiencing unconditional love. The better way for me to phrase that sentence would have been to say, "I am working toward becoming a high-value woman who attracts high-value men."

Clear the Clutter!

I remember when the Style Network first came on TV. One of its most popular reality series was a show called *Clean House*, hosted by Niecy Nash. Niecy Nash and her crew of designers, organizers, and builders would visit an American family in need of a hoarding intervention. The homes featured on the show were full of clutter, dirt and grime, and furniture that was taking up far too much space, making the environment unlivable. The crew would go through each living space, suggesting what needed to be kept, sold at a yard sale, or tossed in the trash. After a few days, the family would return to an organized and renovated home.

When I think of mental clutter, I think about the messy homes I would see on *Clean House*. Instead of it being physical clutter, mental clutter is made up of emotional baggage, destructive habits, unresolved trauma, and self-limiting beliefs that are running rampant in your mind. Mental clutter could also be the result of thoughts that:

- Do not help you become a better version of yourself
- Make your past seem more real than your present experience
- Trigger self-doubt, anxiety, stress, or fear
- Keep you stuck in old patterns or cycles
- Cause you to mismanage your time

Similar to how a cluttered home soon becomes unlivable, a cluttered mind can make it difficult for you to think clearly, make good decisions, or cope with stressful situations. Imagine you were entering a home full of ornaments that came up to your knees and your task was to find your car keys. How long do you think it would take you to locate your car keys? Where would you even begin to look? When your mind is cluttered, even the simplest of tasks can feel overwhelming. Since there is a lot of activity happening in your mind, you have little to no energy to invest in your daily obligations. You might set goals for yourself but due to the mental clutter that lowers your mood and causes you to carry a weight of negative energy, you aren't able to follow through with them.

When mental clutter is not properly dealt with, it can become an addiction. Think about the hoarders who find it near impossible to get rid of any of their ornaments even though they provide no value. The low moods and self-limiting beliefs that follow you on a daily basis aren't useful to who you desire to become, yet they somehow fill an empty void. As destructive as they are, they have become part of your survival guide for life; your blueprint for how to protect

MARIAH GISCOMBE

yourself against experiencing more hurt. For example, thinking that you are not worthy of love is a destructive belief, but guess what? It protects you from opening your heart again and possibly experiencing rejection.

Therefore, as much as you would want to get rid of your mental clutter, you must acknowledge the dependency you have on it. Yes, it hurts to think less of yourself, but go deeper and figure out what this self-limiting belief may be protecting you from. It could be protecting you from rejection, abandonment, embarrassment, or failure.

You are the only person who knows the significance of your mental clutter and why you have held onto self-destructive habits and beliefs for so long. No one else will understand the sense of security you derive from being a wallflower, always standing on the sidelines of life and watching everyone else take huge strides. No one else will understand the attachment you have to harmful habits or how your pessimistic thoughts help you make sense of the world.

Just like the hoarder who tears up after letting go of what others might describe as junk, letting go of your mental clutter is a deeply personal and difficult undertaking that forces you to come face-to-face with the negative energy, beliefs, patterns, and behaviors you have clutched onto for so many years.

Nonetheless, as attached as you may be to your mental clutter, it is imperative that you get rid of it in order to live an empowered and awakened life. There are a few questions you can ask yourself to identify what you consider mental clutter:

16

1. What is not working well in my life right now?
2. What are some of the recurring negative thoughts I experience regularly?
3. What are some phrases I constantly repeat to myself?
4. What behaviors consume a lot of my time but don't serve a purpose?
5. What are some of the strong emotions I feel whenever I get triggered?

Signs of a Cluttered Mind

Mental clutter is the unwanted thoughts about yourself or your life that live rent-free. Whether you want to or not, you find yourself gravitating to these harmful or discouraging thoughts on a regular basis. And since you are constantly thinking about these thoughts, you subconsciously empower them and cause them to multiply and influence how you behave and what you believe about yourself. The first step in eliminating mental clutter is learning how to recognize it. When you can identify a negative thought, for example, you can catch it before it starts to spiral and trigger fear or anxiety. Here are some of the signs of a cluttered mind:

1. Excessive Worry

Worry in and of itself is normal. It is normal to feel unsettled about your financial situation, feel nervous about taking on a new opportunity or have concern for a loved one. Worrying only becomes harmful when it becomes compulsive and gives life to irrational fears. For example, when you are constantly tormented by thoughts of not being able to pay your bills, the risk of losing your job if the economy turns for the worse, or the possibility of getting a chronic illness, you are unable to focus on what is real or the things you can control.

Worrying about the economy, for instance, is an unproductive thought because you have no control over the economy—you only have control over what you do with your time, how you spend or save your money, and how you capitalize on your skills and talents. Worrying doesn't give you more control over your future. Instead, it makes you feel anxious about the future and could lead to you taking a passive approach in your life. Worrying causes you to focus on what you can't do, what you can't have, and all of the obstacles (whether real or imagined) that are standing in your way. Focusing on your limitations doesn't help you move forward or see your circumstances clearly. Therefore, getting rid of worry is the first step in liberating and clearing your mind.

2. Guilt or Preoccupation With the Past

Guilt keeps the door to your past open. The "should haves" that arise in your mind every so often cause you to desire to relive your past again. Perhaps you want to mend broken past relationships, take back the time you wasted on an unfulfilling job, or offer an apology for your unbecoming behavior. While it is good for you to feel convicted in your heart of the poor decisions you made in the past, it is unproductive for you to ruminate on what you could have done better.

The reason time is more valuable than money is that once time has been spent, it cannot be returned. Your past is behind you, and so are all of the mistakes or painful experiences that have occurred in your life. The best way to make up for what you didn't do or what you never received in the past is changed behavior. The cycle of guilt ends when you take control of the time you have right now and live your life as your Higher Self—the self that accepts what is and makes every effort to live intentionally.

3. Feeling Demotivated

One of the clear signs of mental clutter or emotional baggage is feeling demotivated. You may be going ahead with your daily routines but find yourself doing tasks passively. Think of a child dragging their feet in a mall, completely disinterested in running errands with their mother. In other words, you are physically present but your mind has checked out. When there are a lot of thoughts weighing heavily on your mind, you can get distracted easily and lose focus on what you are currently working on. At work, your productivity may lag and at home, you may isolate yourself from others or lose interest in your hobbies. Feeling demotivated can be a form of self-sabotage because it causes you to invest little time and effort in what you set out to do. As a result, you fail to reach milestones, follow through with your plans, or remain resilient during difficult times.

Excessive worry, guilt, and feeling demotivated all lead to one thing—the lack of clarity in your thoughts. When you are unable to think clearly, you can make poor decisions concerning your life. Your unregulated thoughts have the power to distort how you perceive your circumstances, making you react impulsively to situations rather than thinking about the best ways to respond. For example, an anxious thought fueled by worry can raise your stress levels, cause your body to go into survival mode, and make you react as though you were in great danger, even though in reality there is no danger. In summary, you will know you have a cluttered mind when you find yourself being controlled by your thoughts and emotions, rather than being the one who controls your thoughts and emotions.

Activity: What Is Your Self-Worth Story?

If you were to describe yourself to someone, what would you say? Out of all the things you could possibly mention about yourself, what would be the top five things that describe who you are? What is the tone of your story? Are you the lead or part of the supporting cast? Are you an overcomer or the victim of circumstance?

Write down your story without overthinking what you want to say. When you are done, read your story aloud and determine whether or not it aligns with the goals and desires you have for your life. Remember that your story is continually being written. In a year's time, it might not be the same as it is today. Therefore, see your self-worth story as a marker of where you are on your transformational journey and the distance you still need to travel to become who you desire to be.

CHAPTER 2:

Getting to the Root of Your Issues

Your willingness to look at your darkness is what empowers
you to change.
– Iyanla Vanzant

O ver the years, how you perceive yourself and what you make of the world has changed. This is because with age and experience comes fresh insight. Ideally, you would want to become a better version of yourself each year, as you gain more wisdom and understanding. However, life wasn't meant to be experienced that way.

Believe it or not, the twists and turns that you have encountered in your life were intentional. This doesn't mean that you deserved to feel pain or experience loss, but that through your hurtful experiences you can build and strengthen your character.

To live a meaningful life isn't to walk in perpetual darkness or live as though you were floating on clouds. You were not built for pain, nor were you built for purely pleasure. The true meaning of life lies in the significance you derive from your experiences. In other words, it is not what happens to you that defines your life, but what you take away from your experiences.

I know your life hasn't always been an easy journey. There have been times when your thoughts kept you up at night and you didn't have anyone to turn to. As disheartening as life can be, remember that you are not the sum of your experiences. Your experiences were intentionally curated to reveal to you the mighty goddess that lives within you.

Taking a Trip Down Memory Lane

Who you were as a kid and the number of experiences you had, has a lot to do with how you view life as an adult. Even though you can learn new skills and knowledge as an adult, your self-concept—how you see yourself—is informed by what you saw, heard, and felt growing up. If your self-concept was never built on a secure foundation, the cracks tend to show up in your adult life. For example, a kid who never felt seen or validated by their parents can grow up to become an adult people-pleaser.

As much as you would like to think that the painful experiences of your childhood get erased from memory as the years go by, the truth is that they don't. Whatever you fail to heal and release, you will end up reliving many years later, until you reach the point of acceptance and surrender.

Not many people enjoy taking the trip down memory lane because, in most cases, it involves confronting deep issues that are buried in the mind. I completely understand the aversion to reflecting on the past. I mean, who would volunteer to relive past painful memories? However, the only way to get over the past and its influence on your adult life is to come face-to-face with it. Instead of looking away or pretending that the pain no longer exists, you commit to understanding what happened to you, why it happened to you, and the impact it has on your life. Let's look at each factor in more detail:

1. What Happened to You?

If you know what happened to you, you can make sense of your experience, according to your own recollection of the event or season. Similar to how you would structure a story, you can create an introduction, body, and conclusion. You can think about how the event or seasons began, how it unfolded, and the manner in which it ended. Giving your story an introduction, body, and conclusion may not reduce the pain of the experience, but it can provide you a sense of closure.

2. Why Did It Happen to You?

After coming to terms with what happened in the past, the next question would seek to understand why it happened. This question is perhaps the hardest to answer, particularly because many times the past event or season was out of control. In other words, the painful experiences you have been through were either a result of human error, human nature, or the unpredictable nature of the universe. For instance, who can explain losing their job due to an economic downturn? Falling sick unexpectedly? Or getting divorced and losing all they had worked for?

The best way to tackle this question is to reflect on the significance of what happened, rather than the actual unfolding of events. Think about the lessons you learned as a result of going through such a tumultuous time in your life. Consider how much personal growth you experienced when all you had to rely on was your effort. Life can seem unfair sometimes, but if you take the time to look at the significance behind your experiences, you will see that life is a blessing. Had it not been for your highs and lows in life, you wouldn't be half of the person you are today. Take a moment to thank God for the mystery and beauty of your life.

3. How Has It Impacted Your Life?

The final question involves being honest with yourself about the ways in which your past experiences have, and continue, to affect your life. Be real about how your current limiting beliefs, fears, or negative self-talk is due to the unfavorable experiences you have been through. It is okay to admit that while you may have made peace with your past, the residue of it still lives on in how you view yourself and others. It is only when you understand the impact of your past that you can begin to take steps to change your self-worth story and commit to improving your mindset and how you live. Your level of self-awareness can also help you get behind your behaviors and motivations so you can get to the root issues and heal your emotional wounds.

Where Your Self-Worth Story Originated From

Children may not be good communicators, but they are excellent imitators. They model the behavior, language, and attitudes of those closest to them as a way of figuring out their place in the world. How you were raised, the words spoken over you, and the cultural expectations you were taught to follow have, to some degree, molded you into who you are today.

As a child, you didn't have any understanding of limitations. In fact, if you were a kid with a vivid imagination, you probably had hopes of one day becoming a real-life superhero! So, where did you learn about what you can't have or what you can't do? There are a number of social environmental factors that have influenced the shaping of your identity. Here are a few to consider:

1. Parental Influence

Do you know who was your first love? Your parents. Depending on who raised you, your mother and father were the first people you laid your eyes on and completely fell in love with. Your survival in this world depended on their unconditional nurturing because you simply couldn't take care of yourself. Nevertheless, although your parents are your first love they can also be responsible for your first heartbreak. When the people you love and depend on the most somehow fail to provide you with the affection, security, and reassurance that you need, they can make you question your own sense of self-worth.

Being given the cold shoulder or being abandoned by your first true love is utterly devastating. As a child, you aren't mature enough to understand that your parents' lack of affection or support is due to their own emotional wounds, not who you are. For example, you might grow up feeling like you are worthless due to your parents projecting their own feelings of inadequacy onto you. Therefore, the relationship you had with your parents growing up set the tone for the relationship you would later have with yourself and how you would relate or attach to others.

2. Teachers and Community Members

Your sense of self-worth was also influenced by factors outside of the home. For instance, the relationships you forged with teachers, church pastors, neighbors, or friends also impacted how you viewed yourself. Every human being has a need for belonging. This need stems from ancient times when the survival of an individual was linked to the survival of the collective. It wasn't possible during the hunter-gatherer days to survive in the wilderness alone. People needed to create communities, which they called tribes so that they could look out for each other. When you feel a sense of belonging to a group of people or a community, you develop a sense of pride in who you are and feel confident about your ability to succeed in the world. However, when you see yourself as an outcast, or someone constantly misunderstood or excluded by others, you can develop an inferiority complex, which encompasses feelings of inadequacy or being less than others.

3. The Media

Nowadays, we learn more about who we are from what we consume in the media. Most of the time, these messages are subliminal, meaning that we are unaware of what we are being made to think or feel about ourselves. The media may or may not have been a major influence on your identity growing up; however, you can't deny how it shapes your desires or creates insecurities in today's times. While the media can be used to bring about a lot of good, it can also indirectly create a lot of pressure for you to conform to societal standards of beauty, success, health goals, relationship goals, and so forth. When you are bombarded with photoshopped images of the so-called perfect life, perfect relationship, or perfect business you can lose sight of your own truth—the truth about who you are and what your purpose is on this earth. The seductive nature of the media causes you to compare your authentic life experience with an illusion of what life is supposed to be like and the unrealistic goals you are supposed to aim for. This proves detrimental to your sense of self-worth because it makes you feel insecure, desperate, or envious of an ideal that in reality doesn't exist.

When you think about who you are, I'm sure you don't consider the role of your parents, community, and the media in shaping your identity. The social-environmental conditioning you have been through has been so subtle that if you don't stop and actually take a moment to think about where your beliefs, attitudes, and behaviors stem from, you wouldn't recognize it. However, since we are in the process of shedding old skin, it's important to explore other factors that have subconsciously impacted who you are.

Activity: Digging Deeper Into Your Issues

Your recurring behavioral issues or limiting beliefs don't just come out of nowhere. If you sit quietly with your thoughts and trace them back to where they come from, you will see that they are connected to past experiences you have been through. For this activity, recall some of your first childhood memories. Relive them in your mind as though you were transported back in time. Notice the reaction these memories send through your body. How do these memories feel? Can you pin an emotion, sensation, adjective, or sound to these memories?

Next, focus on the feelings that arose while recalling these memories. Blow these feelings up in your mind and make them as strong and powerful as you can. You might notice yourself getting uncomfortable, sweating, or tearing up. This is your body's way of cleansing itself of the emotional charge it is carrying.

Before you end the activity, think about a recent situation in your life that stirred up the same emotional reaction you are experiencing. Ask yourself the three questions: *What happened to you? Why did it happen to you? And how did it impact your life?*

This activity aims to show you how early childhood experiences are inextricably linked to adult experiences, and the emotional impact these childhood experiences had on you can still be felt many decades later, even if the context of the situation is different. Healing from the past requires you to frequently make these connections by digging deeper and connecting to the core of your issues.

CHAPTER 3:

Mastering Your Mindset

It's not the load that breaks you down; it's the way you carry it.
— Lena Horne

B reaking old and toxic cycles is never easy. You might be ready for change, but you'll have a hard time convincing your mind that change is what you need. From a biological perspective, humans were never built to embrace change. Change for our ancestors meant confronting danger and risking death, so the more familiar the environment was, the better. We have evolved since then and in modern times, change is synonymous with personal development. Without embracing change, we cannot self-actualize.

Your brain will try and fight every effort you make to change because it is hell-bent on maintaining tried and tested habits, routines, and mental processes. Instead of trying to convince your brain that change is what you need to grow, you need to take a more aggressive approach and subconsciously rewire your brain. You don't need to undergo brain surgery to do this. All you need is to focus on what you feed your brain consistently. In other words, your new mantra ought to be: "I am what I think."

The Reticular Activating System (RAS)

Your brain is the central intelligence system in your body. It is the hub for all your stored and working memory, learned behaviors, and belief system. The only reason you have a conscience is due to the many years of stored data in your brain. At any second, your brain is processing billions of small pieces of data. To undertake this enormous task, it relies on the reticular activating system (RAS), which is made up of a group of nerves located at your brain stem. The job of the RAS is to decide on what information to remember and what information to discard or naturally forget.

For instance, when you get in your car and make your way to work, you aren't thinking about changing the gear lever from one to two, or pushing down on the brake pad when you stop behind another stationary vehicle. The reason you don't think about the process of driving is because it has already been learned and recorded by the RAS.

So, how does the RAS choose what information to store and keep?

The RAS detects the things you pay attention to and assumes that since your mind is constantly focused on a certain number of things or processes, they are worth remembering! However, the RAS has its limitations. For example, it can't decide on your behalf whether a certain habit is "healthy" or "unhealthy." That is a moral decision you need to make. Smoking is technically considered a habit carrying many health risks, but your RAS won't help you break your habit of smoking. It will simply notice the frequency at which you reach out for a cigarette and memorize the behavior. Therefore, the RAS can in some cases work in your favor, and other times it can work against you.

Many years ago, I had a client who scheduled a session with me because she wanted to learn how to develop more confidence in public speaking. When we met up for coffee, I saw a young career woman who was bursting with youthful energy and radiating light. In my confusion, I had to ask her:

"So, what exactly do you want me to help you with?"

"I want to develop more confidence in public speaking," she enthusiastically replied.

"From the looks of things, you are already confident," I said.

"Well... when I'm speaking to a person on a one-on-one basis, I tend to display confidence. However, as soon as I am placed in a boardroom setting with a number of managers or clients, I become quiet like a church mouse!"

I recalled how the RAS works and how it deliberately seeks information that confirms our existing beliefs. My client believed that she wasn't confident speaking in front of a room of people, so guess what? She wasn't! But on the flip side, she believed that when speaking to a person on a one-on-one basis she was confident—and this was true too! In other words, her RAS made her see exactly what she wanted to see, and as a result, it influenced how she carried herself in professional settings.

What do you believe to be true about yourself? Be careful when answering this question as it will reveal how you carry yourself and the parameters you have set in your life. Your subconscious beliefs become your conscious actions the more you focus on certain information. For example, preoccupying your mind with negative information will yield negative beliefs, which will lead to a negative mindset or behaviors. If you desire to become more positive, the last thing you would focus on is negative news, right? Because doing so wouldn't help you adopt positive beliefs. Therefore, all it takes to influence your mind is being aware of what information you feed it.

Retrain Your Brain to Get Out of Negative Patterns

We are all guilty of negative thinking every once in a while. Modern life can be stressful and sometimes our response to stressful circumstances is to resort to negative thinking (try watching an hour of prime-time news and notice the quality of your thoughts after the show has ended).

Negative thinking becomes concerning when it turns into a habit. In other words, when your default response to circumstances—whether good or bad—is to think negatively, then it can lead to other problems, such as low self-esteem, chronic stress and anxiety, or feelings of hopelessness. The key to changing a negative thought isn't piling on more self-criticism and feeling ashamed of your low quality of thoughts. Or deciding to simply ignore a negative thought when it arises, as though it wasn't a product of your own thinking.

Do you want the truth? Here it goes: The best way to get out of negative thought patterns is to accept that you are what you think, and since you are not satisfied with the person your thoughts have shaped you to become, you need to make better choices about what to think and believe. Every thought has a cause and effect. By entertaining a certain caliber of thought, you will achieve certain outcomes or feel compelled to act in certain ways. Thinking that you are not deserving of a promotion at work won't help you get a raise. Instead, it will cause you to feel discouraged about your career development. The same applies if you carry negative money beliefs. Your disempowering thoughts about money won't help you achieve the level of financial freedom you deeply desire.

Therefore, to become a better version of yourself, you need to train your mind to think better thoughts. How do you do this? There are three steps that you can follow to help you think differently:

1. Identify Your Negative Thoughts

Come to terms with the quality of your thoughts. Own the fact that you are prone to making negative assumptions about yourself, your capabilities, or other people. Admit that when you feel stressed or threatened your default is to think of the worst-case scenario and act as though it were true. Here are a few more negative patterns of thinking you may be guilty of doing:

- **Jumping to conclusions:** Without knowing all of the facts, you often make negative assumptions about what others might be thinking or the motivations behind their actions.

- **Overthinking:** You dwell on a negative thought repeatedly, analyzing it from various perspectives, and as a consequence, you end up troubled with fear.

- **Overgeneralizing:** You judge whatever is happening in your current situation based on what occurred in the past. This pattern of thinking can lead to anxiety as you may feel like the past is constantly repeating itself in your life.

- **Labeling:** Based on your weaknesses, you assign labels to yourself that categorize you and make it difficult for you to see yourself any other way. The same negative pattern can also be applied to other people. Based on how others behave, you assign labels to them, which makes it difficult for you to see them in any other way.

- **Emotional reasoning:** This pattern of negative thinking occurs when you assume that something is true based on how you feel about it. For example, if you are afraid of accepting an opportunity, you might interpret your fear as a sign that the opportunity is not good for you or that it carries certain dangers. Meanwhile, your fear might be a result of your aversion to change.

When you have identified your negative thinking patterns, take a moment to accept your negative thoughts for what they are—just thoughts. Your thoughts are not necessarily true reflections of your present reality. They are simply your perceptions about what is true.

2. Reframe Your Thoughts

Remember that you can't "get rid" of your negative thoughts because they are a product of your own thinking. Instead of getting rid of your negative thoughts, you can choose to reframe them, which is to redefine or restructure your thoughts. A simple switch from "can't" to "can" will reframe how you think about a certain thing. For example, you might visit a car showroom and get in the driver's seat of your dream car. Instead of thinking to yourself, "I can't afford this," you could think, "I can have this!" Or when you are tempted to think "I'm unqualified for the job," you can reframe the thought by thinking "I have the potential to succeed at anything I put my mind to." When reframing your thoughts, try to replace them with thoughts that are soothing and compassionate so you can calm your nervous system, reduce stress, and stabilize your moods.

3. Challenge Your Inner Critic

Your inner critic describes the negative internal dialogue you have with yourself. When your inner critic is activated, you may have a tendency to resort to negative thoughts about yourself or others. For instance, your inner critic will try to convince you that your negative assumptions are true or that people are generally untrustworthy. The best way to challenge your inner critic is to ask for evidence to back up these negative claims. Since the inner critic relies on emotional reasoning, most of what it suggests to you isn't based on facts, but pure emotion. It will take advantage of your strong emotions, like anger, and cause you to turn against yourself or other people. Thus, the next time you are harassed by your inner critic, interrupt the negative thought with a question: "I hear what you are saying, but is there any factual evidence to back your claim?"

Banishing Your Negative Thoughts With 3 Expert Techniques

When left to roam, your mind can cause a lot of havoc for you. An ungoverned mind wanders from past to future, avoiding the discipline of being still and present in the moment. How many times a day do you reminisce about the past or worry about your future? And when you do happen to wander off in the past or future, how do you end up feeling about yourself afterward?

The present moment is a gift because it carries with it all its possibilities.

Just let that sink in for a few minutes.

In this present moment, you can do anything you like and you are likely to see immediate effects of your actions. If you wanted to start a business right now, you could put this book down, go online, and begin the registration process. If you feel like meeting new people, you can join an interest-based group on Meetup. Do you miss someone? You can send them a text right now and nothing would stop you!

Now, do you see why a wandering mind can be an act of self-sabotage? When you dwell on the past or spend time thinking about your future, you miss out on the possibilities available to you in this present moment. Add negative thoughts to this, and not only are you dissociated from reality, but you are also reinforcing negative beliefs about yourself and others.

Rewiring my brain was an eye-opening experience. It allowed me to see how I had been giving my power away to toxic thoughts, people, and habits. I saw how much I had been perpetuating my own suffering by living in my head rather than embracing the possibilities laid out before me. So I decided to reclaim my power by unsubscribing from any thought or any person that made me feel afraid of being myself, intimidated by my own potential, and helpless about my future.

I no longer needed others to affirm my calling or remind me that I am worthy of greatness. The empowerment I yearned for had to come from within.

The more I remained present, the happier I became. Of course, I wouldn't have been able to train my mind to stay present without practicing three powerful mind techniques—journaling, affirmations, and meditation. Why are these techniques so powerful? They can help you tap into your subconscious mind and make positive suggestions to your brain. After much repetition, these positive suggestions become ingrained in how you think and feel about yourself, to the extent that it rewires your brain.

I developed a habit of spending time journaling and writing down what I wanted in my life. The act of writing down my goals helped me see the bigger picture of the direction I wanted to take in life. It also made it clearer what I needed to change about my current circumstances in order to achieve my goals. My journaling helped me feel inspired to set a standard for myself and redesign how I lived.

If you were to enter my office, you would see 10 years worth of note-books, loose papers, post-it notes, and letters I wrote to myself to strategize the kind of life I wanted.

Journaling also encouraged me to invest more time in strengthening my spiritual life. Each day, I would jot down prayers for guidance. My prayers were simple but intentional so that I could attract exactly what I desired. One of my prayers was: "God, align me to my Divine path." What I asked for was simple and straightforward, which made it easier to memorize and visualize what my answered prayer would look like. Reading through prayers I wrote many years ago is something I enjoy doing whenever I want to reflect on how far I've come on my journey and the battles I have fought and won thus far.

Creating positive affirmations was a new experience for me. Growing up, I didn't get a lot of positive reinforcement, so having to speak life over myself seemed a bit uncomfortable. It was only after I began reciting positive affirmations that I came to respect the power of words. Not only do words carry life or death in them, but they can also influence your reality.

When I began my transformation journey, I had a controlling and scattered mind that prevented me from fully enjoying my life. Some of the first affirmations I recited were curated to help me achieve mental clarity and shift to a mind of faith where I trusted that I was being guided and supported by a Higher Power to find my way in the world. The power of my affirmations came from repetition. I created alarms during the day where I would stop what I was doing, close my eyes, and recite an affirmation. Sometimes, I would even go as far as challenging my inner critic with a positive affirmation about myself or my capabilities.

And lastly, I developed a practice of meditating. Meditation is a spiritual practice that has helped me quieten my mind, increase my level of self-awareness, and make positive suggestions to my subconscious mind. There are many forms of meditation and many different kinds of meditative techniques to choose from. Moreover, besides using meditation to connect to my inner power, I also use it when I want to relax my body and declutter my mind. Meditation was, and still is, a fundamental part of my journey. It helped me realize that most of what I felt threatened by were illusions in my mind; ungoverned thoughts that were running around and causing havoc. Meditation has helped me separate what is real and occurring in the present moment and what is merely a perception or a fear-based belief.

Activity: Meditation for Releasing Troubling Thoughts

Get yourself in a comfortable position, either on a chair or on the floor. Make sure your back is straight, shoulders relaxed, and arms resting on your lap. Close your eyes and focus on your breathing. Notice the subtle changes in the pace and rhythm of your breathing. Feel your chest expand as you breathe in and gently collapse as you empty your lungs of air.

When you are feeling relaxed, imagine that you are given access to your mind. As you travel deeper into your mind, you see your troubling thoughts floating like clouds. Some of these thoughts you know very well and others you have never experienced before. Now imagine that each troubling thought makes its way toward you, in slow motion, seeking acknowledgment.

As each thought slowly approaches you, you are able to take a good look at it and see it from multiple angles. If you need more time to look at each thought, you can slow the pace at which it travels even more. As you observe each troubling thought, ask yourself questions about the nature of it:

- What am I looking at?
- How many ways can I look at this?
- What is the intention behind this thought?
- What message or lesson can I take from it?

As the thought comes closer, imagine it becoming more powerful in your mind. Your mind is completely wrapped around this single thought and you have full awareness of what you are looking at. Take a deep breath and as you inhale, embrace the troubling thought as a part of you. After all, it is the product of your own mind. As you embrace the thought, feel its power diminishing slowly, until it no longer overpowers your mind. Imagine its power becoming so small that the thought evaporates into thin air.

You are now one with your troubling thoughts and there is no need to resist it any longer.

Now, follow the same process with the other troubling thoughts you have floating in your mind. Focus on one thought at a time until there are no more troubling thoughts to acknowledge. When you are ready to end the mediation, take a few deep breaths and open your eyes.

COMMITMENT #2:

Prioritize Your Self-Care

CHAPTER 4:

Nurturing the WHOLE You

I define joy as a sustained sense of well-being and internal peace – a connection to what matters.
— Oprah Winfrey

This section of the book might feel uncomfortable to you because I'm delving into self-care. I know, I know—you barely have time for self-care, but allow me to explain why it is a necessity.

Forget about the commercials on TV that advertise scented candles and call that self-care. While I love scented candles, they have nothing to do with taking care of yourself. Nurturing who you are is not about indulging in food or spoiling yourself with a new pair of shoes. It is a lot more significant than that.

Don't allow the culture of consumerism to make you think that your worth is determined by what you buy.

The real meaning of self-care is preserving or maintaining your well-being. It is about protecting your peace, cultivating your own happiness, and responding to your physical and psychological needs. In essence, anything that you do to show compassion and consideration for yourself is an act of self-care.

You have always considered the needs of others above your own. It shows that you have a big heart and that is something we hardly see in others nowadays. But how effective can you be in serving others when you haven't fulfilled your needs first? When you make your well-being a priority, you strengthen your mind, body, and soul allowing you to show up as a *whole* being in the world, ready to share your light with others.

Energy and the Body

Do you remember biology class back in school, where you learned about the anatomy of the human body? What did your teacher say about the body's need for energy? Can you recall?

Let me summarize it briefly for you. The human body cannot function without energy because energy is the fuel it needs to perform bodily functions, like sleeping or talking. The main source of energy for your body lies in the compounds found in food. These compounds are broken down and used to maintain the health of your cells and tissues, repair muscles, and power vital organs like the brain and heart.

For the most part, when people hear the phrase, "protect your energy," they think that it refers to this particular process of conserving your body's energy supply. However, if you hang around people who are on their journey of awakening, you will hear this phrase being spoken about in a different context. From a spiritual perspective, the body is sustained by life force energy.

How different is this from the energy sourced from food?

Life source energy is "Divine energy"—the One energy that created all things. Everything that exists in thought, object, plant, animal, or human form is made from Divine energy. Some people personify this energy and believe that it is a Higher Being, while others choose to see it as spiritual power, high vibrations, consciousness, or universal love. As you continue awakening, you will intuitively sense what life source energy means for you.

Now we can look at the phrase "protect your energy" again with life source energy in mind. There are two main realms, or worlds, of existence: the physical and spiritual realm. Life source energy is part of the spiritual realm; however, it is responsible for creating all other realms, including the physical realm. In other words, you exist because of a divine entity, spirit, or power that called *you* into being.

Nevertheless, each realm has its own laws that govern how it functions. For example, in the physical realm, we have the law of gravity that determines the weight of the human body and keeps us physically grounded on the earth. The law of gravity doesn't apply in the spiritual realm because there aren't any physical objects there—everything in the spiritual realm is energy or spirit.

This also means that for life force energy to exist in the physical realm, it needs to inhabit physical objects or bodies so it can be transferred from one physical entity to another. The human body, therefore, serves as a switchboard between the physical and spiritual realm.

A great analogy to use here is the process of electricity moving from the substation to your home. When you put on your electric stove, you don't physically see the electricity, do you? But judging on the heat produced in your food, you know that electricity is there. If you were to make contact with a pure electric current, you would get electrocuted because when any form of energy isn't properly handled it can bring a lot of danger. Your home's switchboard distributes electricity into different circuits for various living spaces in your home. The switchboard is what allows energy into your home without you having to get in direct contact with electricity.

Your body is the switchboard allowing life force energy access into the physical realm. Besides connecting you to life force energy, your body can also absorb other kinds of energies, like negative energy received from another person. The kinds of energies your body welcomes in can affect your mind, body, and soul. For example, a child who grows up being told they are never going to amount to anything absorbs the negative energy released by their parent. If the energy isn't cleared or released, it creates an energy block. Wherever there is a block, there is a barrier, meaning that life force energy cannot flow through properly. As a result, the child may grow up with psychological issues like a low self-esteem, emotional wounds that wear their soul, or physical illnesses like anxiety or depression.

Let's look at another example. Someone who spends most of their time around an angry person will eventually adopt the same temperament as that person. How does this happen? Unknowingly, they can absorb the same energy governing the other individual's behavior, which means that after some time, they will start to exhibit similar tendencies, like yelling, throwing accusations, or being aggressive when provoked.

Protecting your energy is, therefore, about regulating what kind of energies you give access to your body. Of course, you will certainly want to give access to life force energy because that is the energy connected to growth, positivity, healing, unconditional love, fertility, and creativity. However, there are some energies that don't come bearing good gifts. These energies—which are always negative—come to suck the life force out of you, lower your mood, and cause you to drag your feet through life. You should be careful not to allow these energies to enter your life, but if they do, be sure to clear and release the blocks.

The High Cost of Not Caring for Your Body

As someone who is highly sensitive, people loved being around me because without them even asking I would skillfully intuit their needs. I was a user's dream friend and a narcissist's dream girl! I had no understanding of energy at the time and had no idea that I was literally siphoning my life force's energy away.

It was draining me slowly and making me sick.

I had reached extreme burnout and started experiencing symptoms of depression. Around that time, I stumbled on a book called, *Women's Bodies, Women's Wisdom: Creating Physical and Emotional Health and Healing* by Dr. Christiane Northrup (Northrup, 2020). In the book, Christiane discussed how women were coming into her practice with all sorts of women's health issues, and even after she would suggest conventional therapies and surgeries, more often than not their issues and symptoms would come right back.

She began to ask her clients, "What is your body telling you that you need right now?" The responses would be things like:

- "I need to quit my soul-sucking job"
- " I need to get a divorce"
- "I need to find my purpose"

After encouraging her patients to follow their internal prompt-ings, she said that her clients' bodies would begin to heal themselves. Blown away by the results, she completely changed her practice and became a holistic women's health specialist instead of practicing conventional medicine.

My life was completely changed after reading her book. I began researching the mind-body connection, which sent me on a healing journey of my own. I learned about the body's energy centers (i.e. Chakras) and uncovered that in many ways being a people-pleaser was literally making me sick, depleting my energy, and killing me slowly.

This is what led me to commit to prioritizing myself and my self-care. I could no longer "put up" with anything that didn't make me feel alive. I took a sabbatical from my consulting business in 2018, after feeling drained and burned out. I also took out a piece of paper and created what I call "Optimal Health Action Steps." I stuck the piece of paper on my fridge and began tackling each item over the course of several months.

Here is what I wrote:

1. Remove dairy, meat, soy, eggs, processed foods, and fast food from my diet.
2. Drink 2 liters of water per day.
3. Purchase organic produce (using the dirty dozen/clean fifteen guidelines).
4. Remove or distance myself from people carrying toxic energy (this included severing toxic relationships with some close friends and family).
5. Remove any impediment to good sleep.
6. Improve my home's air quality with filters, plants, and salt lamps.
7. Sweat (through exercise).
8. Do yoga daily.
9. Stay meaningfully connected with those who love, support, and honor me.
10. Incorporate intermittent fasting.

As a result, I began having sharp mental focus and more stable moods, which were also positively influenced by the fact that I was in the best physical shape I had ever been and had pain-free menstruations. Making these lifestyle changes also helped me develop a greater appreciation for my body and experience high energy throughout the day.

Strengthening the Mind-Body-Soul Connection

Get yourself in a comfortable position and close your eyes. For the next five minutes, I invite you to focus on your breathing. Notice the particular rhythm of your breathing, the length of each inhale and exhale breath, and the release of tension as you bring down your heart rate.

Now tell me, how do you feel? Describe your emotional state in a word. Next, tell me what kinds of thoughts are going through your mind. Describe the quality of your thoughts. When you are ready, you can open your eyes.

After performing this simple exercise, you may notice a few things. First, your body may feel lighter and your muscles relaxed. Second, your mood and energy may have increased during the exercise, which would lead to the third change—the improved quality of your thoughts. This exercise clearly shows the mind-body-soul connection. Your physical well-being is connected to your mental and psychological well-being. When your mind, body, or soul is in poor shape, you can experience physical disease or psychological "dis-ease."

Take my long battle with health issues for example. If I had visited a traditional doctor, they would have prescribed pills to treat my physical symptoms or recommend surgery to remove the physical ailment. Even though this solution would solve my physical discomfort, it wouldn't get to the root of the problem. You see, my health issues were a byproduct of my physical, spiritual, and psychological environment. My physical illness was my body's way of alerting me that the food I was eating wasn't providing me sustenance, the people I had allowed in my space weren't nurturing my development, and my mental health was slowly deteriorating.

Learning about the mind-body-soul connection caused me to understand that I was a multi-dimensional being. I was more than my physical body and much more than my thoughts and feelings. Many of us have only ever developed one aspect of who we are, like taking care of our physical body, and neglected to build a relationship with other aspects of ourselves. Eventually, neglecting parts of who we are catches up to us because unless we embrace the fullness of who we are, we cannot feel whole.

So, what does a healthy mind-body-soul connection look like? As mentioned above, I completed my Optimal Health Action Steps to strengthen my mind-body-soul connection. I wrote down actionable steps that I could turn into positive habits and integrate into my lifestyle. My list addressed the imbalance I found in my own life and the personal steps I was willing to take. When you seek to strengthen your mind-body-soul connection, your Optimal Health Action Steps will look different from mine. They will reflect the imbalance you find in your personal or professional life and list steps you are comfortable taking to achieve wholeness.

Here are a few suggestions on the areas you can focus on to improve your mind-body-soul connection:

1. Mind

To strengthen your mind, you can focus on these areas:

- Decision-making skills
- Emotional regulation skills
- Memory and concentration

2. Body

To strengthen your body, you can focus on these areas:

- Healthy eating (focusing on whole, plant-based foods)
- Active lifestyle
- Sleep

3. Soul

To strengthen your soul, you can follow on your psychological and spiritual well-being:

- Building emotional resilience
- Practicing gratitude
- Creating and forcing healthy boundaries

How to Reverse the Signs and Symptoms of Burnout

Burnout is one of the common side effects of a mind, body, and soul imbalance. It causes physical, mental, and emotional exhaustion to the extent that you may feel like your body is shutting down. When left unchecked, burnout can sap your energy and make it difficult for you to live a full and vibrant life. However, you don't have to reach this stage if you know how to detect burnout during its onset. When you are on the way to burnout, you are likely to experience the following symptoms:

- **You have lost interest in your day-to-day routine:** Every day looks and feels the same. You are no longer energized to go to work, see your friends, or spend time on your hobbies.
- **You have become apathetic:** You aren't emotionally stirred by anything, or feel any motivation to invest in your goals or improve your well-being.
- **You are always tired, even after a good night's rest:** You may notice that you wake up feeling drained and continue throughout the day with low energy. You feel like spending the entire day on the couch doing nothing.
- **You don't find meaning in what you do:** Although you may be working, you don't find your work meaningful. You can't seem to find anything that makes you feel glad for being alive.

It is important to note that feeling tired isn't necessarily a sign that you are approaching burnout. It is normal to go without quality sleep for a few days, experience body aches and pains, or go through a season where you feel demotivated. However, if you feel like this for an extended period of time, it may be a sign of burnout. When it finally kicks in, burnout doesn't hit you all at once. It occurs gradually and can be subtle at first. If you pay attention to the state of your mind, body, and soul, you may be able to detect when you are experiencing burnout.

There is also a difference between feeling stressed and experiencing burnout. When you are stressed, you feel a lot of pressure due to the increasing demands in your life. The stress you may be feeling may put physical or mental pressure on you, causing you to go into fight, flight, or freeze mode. During fight mode, you may react impulsively, taking what others say or do at face value or perceiving their actions as attacks. In flight mode, you may isolate yourself from others so you can reduce the amount of stimuli around you and calm your nervous system. And when you are in freeze mode, you may go numb, feel stuck, procrastinate, or find it difficult to think clearly and make good decisions.

Burnout isn't the same as feeling stressed. When you have burnout you are running at a mental, physical, and emotional deficit. You experience a lack in most areas of your life. Nothing that you do feels fulfilling, which makes you feel empty. While you can turn a stressful situation around by regulating your emotions and adopting better coping strategies, when you have burnout you don't see any hope of things turning around.

The good news is that burnout is reversible, but it requires you to take the "Three R" approach: Recognize, reverse, and resilience. Below is a breakdown for each step:

1. Recognize

The first step is to recognize when you are feeling the effects of burnout. By recognizing when you are fatigued or have lost passion for your life, you are able to look for the physical, mental, or emotional triggers that have led you to that point. A simple way to gain more awareness of your bodily sensations and symptoms is to practice doing body scans. Close your eyes and take a few minutes to direct your attention to each part of your body, from the crown of your head to the soles of your feet. As you scan each body part, look for any signs of tension or discomfort (these could be signs of stress). The more you practice doing body scans, the easier it will be to notice sudden changes to your physical and psychological well-being.

2. Reverse

If you detect burnout when it is too late, you would need to reverse the effects of burnout. The aim is to focus on actionable steps that can end the cycle of stress, lethargy, or overthinking. Unless you make a concerted effort to act in ways that are contrary to how you are feeling, your body will grow accustomed to the symptoms of burnout and it will be a lot harder to unlearn certain self-destructive or unhealthy behaviors and attitudes. The action you take to reverse burnout doesn't need to be big; however, it must be directed at the cause of your burnout.

For example, if your burnout was caused by a stressful work environment, you would need to start looking for a job in another company or speak to your HR manager and ask to switch teams or departments. The action you take should bring instant relief and create a barrier between you and your stressor. If the cause of your burnout is more complex, like being in a toxic codependent relationship, then your reversal plan would need to have several actionable steps to untangle yourself from the stressor. One of the steps, for example, could be to speak to a counselor or life coach and get third-party advice.

3. Resilience

Preventing burnout should be your number one goal. One of the best ways to prevent burnout is to develop resilience. Resilience is the ability to withstand difficulties and maintain a leveled mind. Let's face it—life is unpredictable and as much as you try to live a stress-free life, there will always be situations every once in a while that trigger your stress response. To improve your resilience, you can practice the three techniques mentioned in Chapter 3.

Activity: 30 Day Energy Detox Challenge

Every once in a while your body needs a detox to cleanse your gut and rev up your digestive system. The purpose of detoxifying the body is to remove the harmful metals and food waste that could make you sick or cause unwanted diseases. Similarly, your body needs a spiritual detox, every so often, to remove negative energy, clear blocks, and ensure that life force energy is flowing through you. If you are in need of an energy detox, you can take the 30 Day Energy Detox Challenge.

The rules of the challenge are simple: for 30 days, avoid exposure to toxic energies. What are some of the sources of toxic energy? Here is a list of possible sources of toxic energy that you can refer to:

- Social media.
- Manipulative, judgmental, or pessimistic people.
- Limiting beliefs and negative thought patterns.
- Unresolved emotional trauma.
- Polluted air or cluttered living spaces.
- Negative news or gossip.

The aim of this challenge is to see how long you can go without being influenced by negative energy. Don't feel bad if you aren't able to remain free of toxic energy for the entire 30 days. See it as a learning curve and attempt to do the challenge again, until eventually, you make it to day 30.

CHAPTER 5:

Learning to Say No

You wanna fly, you got to give up the sh*t that
weighs you down.
— Toni Morrison

T here is something that every healthy relationship has in abundance—respect. Respect is acknowledging the humanity of another person and considering their needs and wishes. When there is a sturdy foundation of respect in a relationship, parties are able to build trust, communicate openly, and support each other.

It is a sad reality that in most of our relationships we don't demand respect. This is especially true in close relationships with friends and family. We give those we love a free pass to treat us any way they like, believing that it is who they are. As a consequence of not demanding respect from others, we often feel unseen, misunderstood, and taken for granted.

How a person treats you has a lot to do with what you allow. If you give others a free pass to speak to you carelessly or violate your boundaries, they will learn that that kind of behavior is acceptable.

Respect isn't something you deserve. It is an essential need. It is what helps you feel that you belong and that your thoughts and feelings matter.

Your Standards Aren't High Enough

Did you know that within seven seconds of meeting a person, they have already created an impression in their minds about who you are? This impression informs how they speak to you, the kind of topics they are open to discussing, and whether or not they can respect you. In most cases, you are not aware of how another person perceives you and whether you have passed or failed their evaluation until they start showing you through their attitude.

The only way to manage how others perceive you is to work on improving how you perceive yourself. As much as you would like to believe that your fears and insecurities are hidden, they tend to show up in how you carry yourself. When you don't value your own thoughts and feelings, others will know in the way you speak about yourself. Similarly, when you don't respect your own time and commitments, you certainly won't see the need of respecting other people's time and commitments either.

The solution to gaining respect from others isn't about manipulating how others see you, but instead working hard on raising your own personal standards. When a person sees that you are confident and hold high standards for yourself, they are likely to respect you.

Your personal standards are the reasonable expectations, values, and life principles you live by and hold others accountable to. When you have high standards, you require others to treat you with the highest regard. Asking to be treated with the highest regard is a sign of self-respect, not arrogance. The definition of arrogance is thinking highly of yourself and looking down on others. This isn't the same as showing self-respect. An arrogant person may have high standards but the intention behind them is to feel worshiped by others.

Self-respect is a sign of healthy self-esteem. Since you value your thoughts, feelings, and decisions, you expect others to respect them too. People don't need to agree with you or see life from your perspective, but you still expect them to accept who you are and give you the room to be yourself. Having low standards is a sign of low self-esteem. Due to not seeing the value in who you are, you have low expectations of how others should treat you. Similar to how others can pick up on your high standards, they can also sense when you have low standards. How do they do this? They see how easily influenced you are by their many suggestions, the kinds of behaviors you accept, and whether or not you stand up for your values and beliefs.

Your standards aren't only reflected in your relationships. They can also be seen in the quality of your work, the quality of self-care you give yourself, and in habits like punctuality and cleanliness. If you live in a disorganized space, for example, it can show the kind of low standard you have set at home. Being late to meetings or submitting work past the deadline could show the kind of low standard you have created at work. In essence, your standards are constantly on full display and evident across several aspects of your life.

3 Steps to Raise Your Low Standards

Some women pride themselves in being "low maintenance," however, I believe that in some cases this is a cover up for having low standards. In the dating scene, a woman who tells a man that she is low maintenance is sending him the message that she doesn't have a lot of expectations for how she desires to be treated, which causes her to settle for less than what she deserves.

Contrary to what many believe, it isn't a badge of honor to be low maintenance, especially if you are a woman who prioritizes self-care. If you honor your physical, psychological, and spiritual well-being, you won't accept poor treatment that would put your health in jeopardy. The truth is that a confident woman is high maintenance, but again, this doesn't mean she is arrogant. What it means is that she has a clear understanding of her goals, principles, and beliefs and will choose to hang around people who are willing to respect her boundaries.

If you are still wondering whether your personal standards are low or high, here are four indicators of having low standards:

- **You agree to things to avoid confrontation.** When someone treats you in a way that isn't respectful, kind, or considerate, you shrug it off or develop a grudge instead of confronting them about it. You act as though you aren't bothered because you don't want to offend the other person.
- **In relationships, you are always the person making compromises.** Amongst your friends or family, you are

known to be the one who ends up going along with the general consensus. You want others to feel comfortable around you, but usually, that means inconveniencing yourself.

- **You esteem others more than you esteem yourself.** When you think of the network of people you know, you feel privileged to be surrounded by people you perceive as smart, beautiful, and successful. You put others on a pedestal and learn to put their needs before your own. When those you esteem treat you poorly, you excuse their behavior because you value your relationship more than your own boundaries and principles.
- **You play the role of caretaker but don't expect to be taken care of in return.** Whenever someone needs a favor from you, you drop everything you are doing so you can be there for them. In extreme cases, you sacrifice your own credit, time, and plans to accommodate others. As generous as this may be, you don't allow others the opportunity to support you when you are in need.

Fortunately, when you identify low standards in your life, you can raise them by adopting new behaviors. Here are three steps you can follow to begin expecting more from yourself and others:

1. Create a Goal Post

When raising your standards, you need to think about what having higher standards would look like for you. For instance, what kind of mindset do you desire to adopt? How do you want people to treat you? And what type of work ethic do you desire? When you visualize having higher standards, you create a goal post that helps you transform your life. Here are a few more questions you can ask yourself when creating your goal post:

- What do I want to achieve in my life?
- Who do I need to become to achieve this?
- What personality traits would I need to cultivate to achieve this?
- What kinds of relationships would I need to build to support this?

2. Get Real With Yourself

After you have created your goal post, you need to assess your current life situation and determine what needs to change in order for you to raise your standards. When reflecting on your life, avoid being judgmental about your actions and behaviors. Simply notice what isn't working and what you need to improve upon. Think about the current standards you have related to your work, health, finances, and relationships. Assess if they are suitable to help you reach your goal post. If they are not suitable, think of ways you can improve your standards or raise your expectations.

3. Find People to Emulate

Raising your standards is difficult when you have never demanded more for yourself. You can make the process less overwhelming by finding people who live by the standards you desire for yourself and emulating them. Emulating someone means to imitate how they behave or the kinds of achievements they have made in their lives. Think of it as drawing inspiration from a mentor or someone who embodies the qualities or lifestyle you admire. Look online on platforms like YouTube for personalities, coaches, or gurus who carry themselves and live by the same principles you seek to adopt.

Drawing the Line With Loved Ones

If a friend mistreated you, over and over again, what would you do? Perhaps at first you would sit them down and explain how their behavior was affecting you, but after some time you would distance yourself from them. There is only so much mistreatment you can take from a friend or colleague before you decide to cut them off.

But what would happen if the mistreatment was from someone you cared about? A spouse, sibling, or parent? We get to choose our friends, but we don't get to choose the families we are born in and the kind of parents who raise us. Setting high standards might work in your friendships or professional circles, but demanding the respect of a family member who is hell-bent on hurting you is a different ball game.

In late 2020, I decided to officially sever ties with several family members. I found comfort and strength in therapy, personal development, and online support groups with other women who shared their experiences of having toxic family dynamics. Being a part of these groups helped me become a better mom to my daughter, Jahniah, and highlighted that for whatever reason, God, the Divine, gave me the responsibility of breaking and healing the toxic generational trauma in my family line.

My daughter is confident, has a supportive tight-knit group of friends, and has a great sense of self—everything I lacked when I was growing up. Being forced to grow up too soon, and at such a young age, caused me to become a conscious parent and provide my daughter with a sense of physical and psychological safety where she knows, without a doubt, that I will always be there at her defense and will always love her unconditionally.

Why You Need Boundaries in Your Close Relationships

As a child, you learned about what was acceptable and unacceptable by taking cues from your environment. If you were raised in a structured environment where you knew what was expected of you and what was deemed unacceptable behavior, you grew up knowing how to distinguish right from wrong. However, if expectations were blurred growing up, or your caregivers were hot and cold when setting rules and expectations, you may have grown up feeling confused on how to distinguish between right and wrong behavior.

A child learns how to build and nurture relationships by modeling the same behavior they see from their parents. For example, if open communication was frowned upon in the parent-child relationship, the child could grow up feeling uncomfortable expressing what they truly think or feel. Or when a child is raised by an emotionally unavailable parent, they may grow up with the subconscious belief that love is earned through self-sacrifice, rather than given unconditionally.

What do your childhood environment and the relationship with your parents have to do with boundaries? Boundaries are the limits or rules that are set to protect individuality in relationships. They help couples, friends, and families differentiate themselves from one another so that their needs, wishes, and beliefs are respected. A child is still too young to understand the importance of maintaining their individuality, therefore, they rely on their parents to teach them how to identify their needs, express their wishes, and honor their beliefs.

When a child is raised by a controlling, manipulative, emotionally detached, or mentally ill parent, they are not taught how to set healthy boundaries. It takes a conscious parent with firm boundaries to acknowledge the need for rules, structure, and limits for their child. Toxic home environments don't have the kind of predictable structures and consistent discipline that children need in order to learn the difference between right and wrong. The lack of proper support structures in these environments could lead to children developing codependency issues, fear of authority or confrontation, or the inability to regulate their emotions and articulate their needs.

Think back to your childhood and the kind of expectations that were enforced in your household. Did your parents create house rules? Did you receive clear instructions of what was expected from you? Do you feel like your parents' discipline was consistent, and that the consequences were fair? Were you taught the difference between right and wrong behavior and given opportunities to learn from your mistakes?

The boundaries you set in your adult relationships are informed by the standards and expectations set in your childhood. If you struggle to stand up for yourself at work or in your romantic relationships, reflect on how this pattern could have stemmed from your childhood. When you were growing up, were you given the platform to voice your opinions? Did you feel heard and accepted by your parents? The good news is that the past doesn't need to repeat itself in the present moment. You can unlearn toxic behaviors from your younger years and adopt new behaviors that support healthy boundaries.

Many adults don't know what healthy boundaries look like because they never saw them growing up. If you have never been in a relationship with healthy boundaries, getting yourself accustomed to them can feel uncomfortable. Due to experiencing blatant disregard for so many years, being in a relationship with someone who respects you can take some getting used to.

However, the most important thing you need to know about healthy boundaries is that you deserve them. Yes—you deserve to feel accepted by those close to you and to freely express your thoughts and emotions without fear of being judged, manipulated, or ridiculed. You deserve to be in relationships where you feel psychologically safe. In other words, you deserve to feel safe being vulnerable with others and opening your heart. Even though you might not always agree with others, you deserve to be in the kinds of relationships where it feels safe to disagree respectfully, where you won't feel like you are stepping on someone's toes by simply sharing your opinions.

Setting boundaries in your close relationships will help you self-differentiate from your loved ones and protect your own interests, needs, and beliefs. Just because you were born in the same family or you are part of the same circle of friends, doesn't mean that you need to think and behave in the same way. Yes, you may be connected by blood or many years of friendship, but your perspective on life and what you desire in your relationships could be different.

When you communicate your boundaries with loved ones, remember that you aren't trying to win them over. Refuse to allow anyone to make you feel like your boundaries are negotiable. You are a sovereign being who has a mind, body, and soul of your own. What you feel is right doesn't need to match the status quo in society or in your family or friend groups. You don't need to get the vote of the majority before you can start living your life the way you envision. Therefore, be firm when drawing limits with loved ones and be consistent in what you deem acceptable and unacceptable behaviors. Your commitment to maintaining your boundaries is what will show your loved ones that you have high standards and won't tolerate just any kind of treatment.

Once you have set your boundaries, the real work begins, which is enforcing them in your relationships. Don't expect every friend or family member to be on board with your new set of boundaries, especially if you previously didn't have any. You will face a lot of resistance when enforcing your boundaries, but that is normal. When people who were used to taking you for granted no longer have the ability to get away with it, they will protest and resist the change. In those moments when you feel like you need to defend your boundaries, take a moment to pause and take a few deep breaths. Remain in your body and emotionally distance yourself from the aggressor. Remind yourself that the outburst or violent resistance is due to the other person's lack of self-regulation. It isn't an indication that your boundaries are unfair, extreme, or punitive.

Give your friends and family time to adjust to your new standards, and don't feel ashamed to distance yourself if being around them causes you to feel intimidated. The first year after setting healthy boundaries will be emotionally taxing, so show yourself compassion and treat each day as an opportunity to learn more about yourself. Whenever you need a gentle reminder about what you deserve, remember these ten statements:

1. It is okay not to be close with your family if it means exposing yourself to negative energy.
2. It is okay to isolate yourself for a weekend and take some time to recharge.
3. It is okay to call people out for not honoring their commitments with you.
4. It is okay not to respond to a text message when you are not in a good emotional space.
5. It is okay to keep aspects of your life private or choose a select number of people to share sensitive information with.
6. It is okay to live a life that people don't understand or may not desire for themselves.

7. It is okay to walk away from a conversation when you feel disrespected.

8. It is okay to ask friends and family members for support.

9. It is okay to block toxic relatives from your social media without explaining yourself.

10. It is okay to say no without making any compromises.

Activity: What's in Your Bubble?

There are certain things you can control and other things that you have no control over. For example, you can't control how someone treats you, but you can control how you respond to their treatment. When setting boundaries, it's important to remind yourself of what you can and can't control. Imagine that you are insulated in a big bubble and the environment within your bubble is in your control. Think of some of the things that would fall within your bubble, such as your attitude, language, decisions, habits, and emotions. When you find yourself being confronted by someone else's opinions or behaviors, imagine them bouncing off your bubble and returning to the sender. If you find yourself triggered by another person's reactions to your boundaries, repeat the following affirmations to yourself:

- I am accountable for my own words and actions.
- I am empowered by the thoughts I have about myself.
- I greet anger/judgment/criticism with love.
- I am unapologetic for saying no.
- My well-being comes first.

CHAPTER 6:

Refilling Your Well

You may not control all the events that happen to you, but you can decide not to be reduced by them.
— Maya Angelou

Reconnecting to who you are isn't a walk in the park. I have often heard it being said over and over again, "Be yourself," but what use is telling someone to be themselves if they have lost sense of who they are?

It might sound strange to you, but I lost touch with who I was in the darkest moments of my life. The pain was the merciless teacher that challenged me to let go of what I thought I knew and search for the deeper meaning of my existence. Don't get me wrong, I am not defined by my pain; however, without having been through soul-wrenching moments, I would have never found my truth.

It was the gift of desperation that made reconnecting to myself possible. If I had not been desperate for peace, real love, and finding my purpose, who knows how different my story would have turned out?

Embrace the season you are in right now because it could be the beginning of your homecoming—returning to yourself after being disconnected for many years. As much as you may think that purpose lies on the other side of your current circumstance, the truth is that your purpose is connected to this very moment too. Who you were yesterday, who you are today, and who you will be tomorrow are all part of your transformation journey.

Take a deep breath and resist the urge to escape this moment. There is healing taking place here, whether you are aware of it or not.

The Valley of the Shadow of Death

In 2012, I was baptized and a few months later, survived sexual assault. The juxtaposition of these two events, and how close they occurred to one another, led to a crisis of my faith. My body was violated and no longer felt like home. I questioned everything I had come to accept as truth, including the meaning of my life. Was I part of a cosmic joke gone wrong?

This painful season ushered me into my "Dark night of the soul" experience where over the course of the next few years, I experienced one hardship after the other. In 2015, I had my breaking point. I couldn't take another day of feeling beaten down. I was tired of rehearsing what happened to me and I no longer found pleasure in picking at my emotional wounds. I was ready to heal and this helped me turn my entire focus on reclaiming my power and consciously becoming a better version of myself. I made the commitment to change my life and the five commitments were the tools and steps that I used to heal, renew my mind, and rediscover who I was.

However, the turnaround didn't come instantly. In fact, the time between deciding to change my life and when I started seeing changes was a journey in and of itself. I learned that healing was a process that I would need to be patient with. During this process, I would experience really high moments and extremely low moments too. This was natural since I was learning and unlearning certain patterns, beliefs, and behaviors. The healing process was also an opportunity to open myself to goodness and love. Did it feel awkward being shown love? Of course, it did! But I had to awkwardly embrace those moments and remind myself that I deserve them.

One of the memories I have during that year was being honored as a "community role model" at the 2015 Black Canadian awards. On my right and left as I sat in the auditorium, were powerful black Canadian movers and shakers from various sectors of society, like the arts, politics, and entrepreneurship. I was dressed for the occasion in a sexy floor-length, high-slit dress, which accentuated every curve and showed off my glowing skin. I topped my outfit with a pearly white smile, which I kept on for the whole night.

This should've felt incredible, right? I mean, being recognized as a role model means that I had been doing something right those past few years! However, I didn't feel as proud of my achievement as I should have. I guess I was suffering from a case of imposter syndrome where a part of me questioned if I really deserved the recognition after everything I had been through. I was so nervous I could barely enjoy my moment in the spotlight because inside I was feeling broken.

It took me many years to confidently admit that I was the fierce and successful woman I thought I was! Finally, I was comfortable with seeing myself happy, being celebrated, or told that I am talented. This transformation came as a result of practicing the five commitments, particularly Commitment #3, which was prioritizing self-care. I had a lot of fun learning about what self-care meant for my well-being and the kind of physical, mental, emotional, and spiritual needs I had been neglecting. My complete wellness became my responsibility. It was something I had control over and could adjust whenever I needed to.

Self-care became a way to refill my well and get to a place where my mind, body, and soul felt whole again. For me, self-care was a deeply personal experience where I got to sow into my own well-being. I didn't make any compromises with my self-care too. I looked for the best products, practices, treatments, and anything that carried a high vibration that I could integrate into my life. A few practices have become my go-to in my self-care regimen. Interestingly, these are also the practices that have held me through this journey of self-discovery and transformation:

- Listening to music
- Going for walks
- Rest
- Prayer
- Meditation

- Hot baths with sea salts
- Hot showers with a coffee scrub
- Facials
- Massages
- Drinking tea
- Affirmations
- Journaling
- Listening to binaural beats
- Spiritual, motivational, and educational books

Self-care remains a priority for me and how I purge my life of toxic energy that seeks to disturb my mind, body, soul, and home environment. The darkest moment of my life, which took nearly 10 years to get out of, ended up becoming the beginning of a new life where I could be the empowered and healed version of myself. Yes, a part of me died the night I was sexually assaulted. However, through that painful death, I was able to give birth to a new identity—the goddess that I am today.

The Pain of Losing Your Identity

Personal identity is the perception you have about yourself and how you describe your life story. It informs how you relate to others, the beliefs you hold to be true, and the meaning you ascribe to your life. It is assumed that when a person comes of age, they already know who they are, but this isn't always the case. Some people aren't aware of who they are or struggle to accept who they are.

In this section, we are not speaking about those people. Instead, we will speak about people who lose their sense of identity after experiencing loss, trauma, or grief. When we think about loss, we often think of it as losing something physical, like financial savings, a loved one, or a job. As painful as it is to lose these tangible things, there is another type of loss that literally changes a person. This is the loss of identity.

If I had to describe what it feels like to lose your identity, I would describe it as being the same as having all of your computer files wiped out by a virus, without any hopes of retrieving them again. The many files, documents, and multimedia that you had spent years organizing under folders are nowhere to be found. When you lose your identity after experiencing pain, it can feel like all of the elements of your personality, aspirations, values, and beliefs have been discarded without any trace of where they went. You have been reset to factory settings and everything you once believed to be true is questionable.

The defenses and boundaries you had built for yourself come crashing down and you feel like a home without doors or windows. You feel exposed, fragile, and afraid of the spaces and environments you used to feel comfortable in. Since identity can be defined in many different ways, it is important for us to discuss the various kinds of losses to identity that you can experience:

1. Relational Identity

Relational identity is the part of you that feels connected to other people. The loss of relational identity is typically felt when grieving a loved one. When you lose someone near and dear to you, it can feel like a part of you has also been taken away. You can also experience a loss of relational identity when roles change within a relationship. For example, a child who is forced to grow up too soon and become the caregiver to their parent can mourn the loss of their identity as a child. As an adult, they may even struggle to define who they are outside of their role as caregiver.

2. Professional Identity

Your professional identity is the self you create based on your profession. Oftentimes, when we introduce ourselves we say, "I am a consultant," or "I am an entrepreneur," as a way to help others make sense of who we are. The loss of a job or retirement can threaten our professional identities. You might wonder, "Who am I apart from being an accountant?" The loss feels significantly greater when you have found purpose in your profession. In other words, not only have you lost your job, but you have also lost the meaning you had ascribed to your life.

3. Spiritual Identity

Every human being has a spiritual identity, but not all of us are familiar with our spiritual identities. For example, if you grew up without being exposed to religion or being taught about spirituality, you may not have awareness of your spiritual identity. Those who experience a loss of spiritual identity are usually people who had cultivated somewhat of a spiritual identity but after a tragic experience felt a disconnect. The loss of spiritual identity stems from questioning the religious or spiritual belief systems one had previously believed to be true. This can be triggered by the death of a loved one, chronic illness, exposure to new information, or feeling betrayed by one's Higher Power. With the loss of spiritual identity comes a collapse of a belief system and the loss of community (those people who shared similar spiritual beliefs as you).

4. Financial Identity

Another way to define who you are is by associating your identity with your social status. When you succeed in life and increase your standard of living, you can modify your character, interests, and lifestyle to match your new social status. You might develop a love for the finer things in life, start family traditions of traveling every summer, and associate with people you perceive to be in the same social class as you. When you experience financial losses, it can affect the identity you had built around the life your money offered you. It can be extremely difficult to separate who you are from your bank account and realize that your worth isn't tied to how much money you make.

Losing your identity is painful because it causes you to question who you are and whether or not what you have believed is a lie. When grief or trauma shakes your belief and value systems, the outlook you have on your life changes. For example, if you had previously valued family, being abused by a family member can make you question the value you place in the family. Your mind may be flooded with questions like, "If a family is supposed to be supportive, why are my parents determined to make my life difficult?" or

"If I am supposed to trust my uncle or aunt, why would they physically or sexually assault me?" When your core values and beliefs are shaken, the only way to pick yourself up is to rediscover who you are—the transformational journey that leads to an awakening.

Forgive Yourself to Heal Yourself

When we process grief or trauma, we tend to focus on staying strong and overcoming the painful experience. This is our way of calming our nervous system and helping our bodies regain a sense of safety. Although it is amazing how quickly we are able to move on after a tragedy, our "dust yourself off" approach doesn't heal the emotional wound that was created.

Do you remember when you would fall off your bike as a kid and would get a physical wound?

The exposed flesh would send shivers down your spine and you would run back inside the house looking for an adult to treat your wound. Leaving the wound exposed for too long would cause an infection and worsen the pain.

How did your caregiver treat the wound? Can you remember?

After cleaning the wound with fresh water or antiseptic soap, your caregiver would cover the wound with a band-aid or dress it with a bandage. Your emotional wounds require a similar kind of treatment in order for them to heal. Instead of leaving the emotional wound exposed by pretending that it doesn't exist or that you don't feel the pain, you need to acknowledge and accept that it is there. Acknowledge the fact that you were a victim of a tragic circumstance that you didn't anticipate and couldn't control. Accept that it happened, but also that it is behind you.

Acknowledging and accepting your emotional wound can help you address the pain you feel when you think back to a dark moment in your life. After some time, you will be able to think or talk about that moment in your life without feeling emotionally triggered—this is a positive sign of healing. Nevertheless, treating your emotional wound doesn't end with acknowledging and accepting what you went through; the next step is to cover the wound with a band-aid, which is forgiving yourself for harboring what was meant to be healed and released.

When you lose your identity after grief or trauma, you can turn against yourself by living in a cloud of shame, guilt, self-sabotage, or self-hatred. You project the strong emotions you feel toward the perpetrator (relative, spouse, boss, or the universe) onto yourself and find ways to harm your own healing process. One of the common emotions a survivor feels after overcoming a traumatic event is shame. Shame can be described as feeling pity, disgust, or humiliation for a wrong behavior. When you feel ashamed of your painful past, you may try to erase it from your memory, feel embarrassed for what you consider foolish or reckless behavior, or feel a sense of pity for your life.

It is difficult to heal an emotional wound when you feel partly responsible for creating it. Moreover, as a form of punishment (a manifestation of self-hatred), you may even desire to keep the wound open and remind yourself of the pain constantly, as a way to "pay" for what you believe was your fault. If you feel this way about your painful past, I encourage you to put down your weapons and recognize the harm you have inflicted on yourself. Notice how the beliefs you have about yourself and the responsibility you feel for your trauma are perpetuating more pain. Turning against yourself isn't the best approach to healing your emotional wound—forgiving yourself is.

Self-forgiveness is a journey all on its own. Unlike forgiving a wrongdoer, when you forgive yourself, you need to wrestle with the negative feelings you have toward yourself. In other words, you need to mediate between the part of you that is ready to heal and the other part of you that is intent on causing more pain. Forgiving yourself takes a great deal of self-awareness and courage. Instead of judging yourself for your past, you seek to understand what happened and how it has impacted you. Doing this helps you own your life story and see your past experiences as being pivotal to who you are today and the woman you are becoming. There are two habits you need to adopt when working toward self-forgiveness: practicing self-understanding and self-compassion. Here is a breakdown of both habits:

1. Self-Understanding

Practice understanding your life experiences and the various events that have either shaped or challenged how you see yourself. Understanding your past isn't the same as agreeing to it or giving those who have hurt you a free pass. You can understand what has happened to you without validating it. In other words, while you don't endorse the trauma you have been through, you have no objections to it either. You can reflect on your past experiences and make sense of them without forming a biased opinion. Here are a few affirmations to help you practice self-understanding:

- I accept who I am.
- I embrace my life story.
- I celebrate my life.
- I am aware of my pain.

2. Self-Compassion

Showing yourself self-compassion is about recognizing you are only human and that you deserve grace as much as anyone else. You have made mistakes in the past and have hurt people just as much as you have been hurt too. It isn't fair to take responsibility for things that were out of your control or to define yourself by your weaknesses or the most humiliating moments in your life. Showing self-compassion will make it easier to reach the point of self-forgiveness and allow your emotional wounds to heal without constantly picking at them. Here are a few affirmations to help you practice self-compassion:

- I care about my feelings.
- I am sensitive to my own needs.
- I extend grace to myself.
- I am at peace with my humanity.
- I am deserving of forgiveness.

Activity: Create a Personal Mission Statement

Think of rediscovering who you are as an opportunity to build yourself into the person you have always desired to be. Since everything you knew to be true about yourself has been reset, you can decide on the kind of physical, emotional, mental, and spiritual well-being you aspire to have.

On a piece of paper, write down ideas or keywords that reflect the kind of woman you desire to be. This woman should be your ideal self, the self that is healed and empowered. Include the things that are essential for you to feel whole, grounded, safe, and nurtured. You can even include health, financial, and relationship goals you aim to achieve. The next part of this activity is to create a personal mission statement that summarizes who you are and how you intend on living your life moving forward, based on the ideas and goals you had written down. Your personal mission statement can be as long or as short as you want it to be. No one else will get to read your mission statement besides you. Print copies of your mission statement so that you can leave them in spaces you frequently visit, like your office, bedroom, or living room. As you continue on your transformational journey, refer to your mission statement and assess how well you are honoring your personal aspirations.

COMMITMENT #3:

Develop Self-Awareness

CHAPTER 7:

Uncovering the Truth of Who You Are

You are on the eve of a complete victory. You can't go wrong.
The world is behind you.
— Josephine Baker

We live in a society that is at war against individuality. Being different nowadays is seen as rebellious or undesirable since it alienates you from everyone else. Let's face it—it is much easier to accept the status quo in your workplace or relationships than to speak up for your needs. But just because it is easier, doesn't make it virtuous.

Empowered and awakened people see the world differently. They tend to see beyond the superficiality of things and desire to live in a truthful way. This often means having to say no when boundaries are crossed, expressing their needs, and distancing themselves from anyone who isn't striving toward unity, peace, and love.

You are not being difficult when you express the truth of who you are and choose to live in a way many people don't understand. You deserve to create the kind of lifestyle that feels like home to you and supports your divine purpose. Never be afraid of walking alone if it means you get the once-in-a-lifetime opportunity to live an authentic life.

What Is Divine Solitude?

How much time do you spend alone? Due to the fast-paced nature of modern society, I assume the answer to that question is "not that much." Solitude is the act of removing yourself from communal settings so you can spend time alone. The purpose of solitude is to recharge and nourish your mind, body, and soul. Nowadays, solitude can be used as a way to seek the presence of the Divine. By removing external stimuli, you are able to focus on your inner life and connect to a deeper part of yourself. The philosopher, Socrates, believed that in his moments of solitude, he would feel the sacred presence of God. During this time alone, he would have fellowship with his *daimon*, representing his divine inner voice.

If you have a rich spiritual life, you will understand what it means to spend time alone with the Divine. However, if you are still getting yourself acquainted with the spiritual realm, then you may wonder what exactly is meant by "Divine solitude." Divine solitude is spending time in the presence of God, or Divine Power. You can do this by engaging in transcendental practices, like prayer, visualization, or meditation. These practices have the ability to activate the parietal cortex–the part of your brain that allows you to have spiritual experiences.

There is nothing you need to do during these quiet moments with the Divine, except for practice stillness. Stillness is the practice of emptying your mind of thoughts so you can reduce mental activity and achieve a state of inner peace. Your Divine solitude will seem uneventful for the most part because instead of focusing on doing, you will focus on being—simply existing in the moment.

The fewer the external and internal distractions, the louder your inner voice becomes. Some call the inner voice the gut feeling, but I like to think of it as intuition. Intuition is the part of you that has access to infinite knowledge, wisdom, and truth. When you are still and your mind is calm, you can intuitively sense and know what you need at that moment. For example, after practicing meditation, you can walk away with a greater sense of clarity about what is truthful and how you ought to move going forward.

How does this relate to uncovering the truth about yourself? When you spend time in the presence of the Divine, you get a break from your thoughts, emotions, and beliefs, and enjoy simply being in the moment. This time spent being present in the moment can help you discover aspects of yourself that haven't been explored, acknowledged, or accepted. For example, after spending time with God, you might discover that your mood swings are due to your high sensitivity, not an attitude problem. You wouldn't get this kind of revelation if you hadn't transcended your everyday existence and activated your intuition. Therefore, the more time you spend alone with the Divine, the greater your self-awareness can grow. Not only can you find out who you are, but you can also find out what is important to you.

Self-Awareness Is the Key

American writer, Audre Lorde, said "Once we recognize what it is we are feeling, once we recognize we can feel deeply, love deeply, can feel joy, then we will demand that all parts of our lives produce that kind of joy" (McLeod, 2021).

What did she mean by this?

Well, to put it simply, the awareness of what you are feeling can teach you more about who you are, how you react to certain situations, and how to improve your sense of well-being. Self-awareness is about asking the many "why" questions about your life to figure out how your experiences have shaped who you are. The point isn't to arrive at any formal conclusion, but instead to gain an understanding of common patterns that have influenced how you feel about yourself, how you relate to others, and how you show up to the world.

Self-awareness won't give you closure from the past, but it will certainly help you piece together how events from your past unfolded and the lasting impact they have made on you. When a client comes to see me, I need to be honest about what I can and cannot offer them during our coaching sessions. For instance, I can't guarantee that after meeting with me for a few sessions the client will eliminate their negative beliefs. As skilled as I am at what I do, I'm not a miracle worker!

I cannot tap into someone else's subconscious mind and reverse years of negative beliefs—only they can do that for themselves. Nonetheless, I can teach the client how to build self-awareness so they can confront their own patterns of thoughts and change them once and for all. Self-awareness is, therefore, the key to healing, but doesn't promise to heal. It allows you to change your habits, beliefs, and life story, but whether you end up doing it or not is your choice.

How to Develop Self-Awareness

Learning how to become self-aware requires introspection. The word *introspection* is derived from the Latin word *introspicere*, which means to observe attentively. When you are introspective, you observe your thoughts and emotions attentively. The aim is to simply look without making any judgments about what you see. By observing your thoughts and emotions, you are able to detect patterns, cycles, and determine the root behind your thoughts and emotions.

Introspection is a valuable practice because it allows you to make informed decisions about your life based on the knowledge you have about yourself and others. For example, after engaging in introspection, you might be convicted about the consequences of a bad habit and put in place strategies that will help you change your behavior. The greater your awareness about how you think and feel, the more control you have over your current circumstances.

Below are three useful strategies to help you develop greater self-awareness:

1. Adopt an Objective Perspective About Your Life

We are all guilty of believing everything we think and feel. In the depths of our despair or frustration, we can feel justified for entertaining certain thoughts and emotions. However, to practice self-awareness we need to start assessing our lives from an objective perspective, which means making an unbiased assessment of our current situation. The trick to adopting an objective perspective on your life is to imagine you were an observer looking into your experience. Imagine you had no affiliation with the people involved, including yourself. From this perspective, assess what is going on without labeling anyone or anything as being "right" or "wrong."

2. Make Self-Reflection a Daily Habit

It can be easier to keep track of our thoughts and feelings when we regularly check in on how we are doing. Self-reflection is the practice of thinking about your life experiences and evaluating your thoughts and feelings. When practiced on a daily basis, you can easily pick up on changes in your mood, sudden onset of stress or anxiety, or emotional triggers rooted in unresolved trauma. Set aside time, either in the morning or in the evening, each day to take note of how you are doing, what you need, and what you are grateful for.

3. Ask for an Assessment From a Trusted Friend

Sometimes, we can get a better understanding of who we are after receiving feedback from others. Since most of the time we are experiencing life from our own perspective, we can be blind to certain behaviors or qualities about ourselves that others can easily pick up on. Find a trusted friend who can provide you with an honest and compassionate assessment of the type of person you are. If you are afraid to meet them in person, you can ask them to send you an email with their feedback. Take in the feedback without feeling the need to defend yourself from whatever they have to say. Remember, they may be observing something that you cannot see for yourself. In your alone time, reflect on the feedback you have received and determine whether it is true and if there is anything you would like to improve on about yourself.

Activity: Take a Psychometric Assessment

Psychometric tests are qualified psychological assessments that can help you understand your natural abilities, skills, temperament, motivation, and behaviors. You are asked to complete a set of multiple-choice questions that seek to explain different aspects of who you are. After taking one of these tests, you can gain better insight into who you are, what motivates you, and how you tend to behave in certain situations. One of the most popular tests focused on increasing self-awareness is the Myers-Briggs test. Take a moment to complete the free Myers-Briggs test online and, afterward, reflect on the results.

COMMITMENT #4:

Connect to Your Inner Wisdom

CHAPTER 8:

Answering the Call

You've just got to follow your own path. You have to trust your heart and you have to listen to the warnings.
— Chaka Khan

My life story, including all of the experiences I had been through as a child, adolescent, and young adult all made sense when I found my calling. You see, at the time, it felt as though the universe was against me. But in hindsight, I can see how each experience was carefully shaping me to become the life coach and healer I am today.

Answering the call on your life is the beginning of an awakening. From that moment onward, your life becomes a vehicle for sharing Divine light with others in whatever manner you choose. You surrender to the flow of your life, moving in the direction you feel led to. For some, this means making a career transition, and for others, it means ending toxic cycles or relationships.

If you have read this far into the book, I believe you are ready for this new chapter in your life; the chapter of growth, healing, and purpose. As uncomfortable as it will be shedding old skin, remember that you have manifested this awakening through your curiosity and desire for a new beginning. Therefore, be kind and patient with yourself during the bumpy journey of your awakening and remind yourself that you were built for this!

The Stages of a Spiritual Awakening

A spiritual awakening is a lot more than being "woke." It entails a complete transformation of your life, including how you see yourself and the new desires, beliefs, and principles you choose to live your life by. Across time and religions, people have had spiritual awakenings which led to a renewed sense of being, therefore, it shouldn't be treated as another new age concept.

In general, there are three questions revisited during a spiritual awakening:

1. Who am I?
2. Where do I come from?
3. Why was I created?

The first question finally puts the issue of identity to rest. The natural stripping away process that you go through during a spiritual awakening causes you to challenge your self-concept, confront the effects of your childhood trauma or conditioning, and uncover your authentic self.

The second question addresses your spiritual heritage. At your core, you are a spiritual being, but where exactly do you come from? Where does your spiritual journey start? How much do you know about your spiritual home? The more you connect to your spiritual self, the greater the clarity you will have about your existence as a spirit. Of course, how you make sense of your spiritual heritage will be different from the next person because there are many different spiritual channels that individuals use. The aim is to find spiritual channels that resonate with you and feel true.

The final question addresses the topic of purpose. When you realize that you were created by a Divine spiritual force, you gain a newfound appreciation for your life. The fact that you are one of the Creator's handiworks means that you were made for a specific purpose, otherwise, you wouldn't exist. Discovering why you were created can also help you make sense of your past experiences, particularly the low points in your life where it seemed as though your life was meaningless. Your purpose reveals that even the darkest moments of your life were a part of your master plan.

A spiritual awakening can be triggered by any significant event in your life, whether it be a bad break-up or losing your job. The nature of the event isn't as important as how the event forces you to reassess your life. For example, for one person, losing their job could lead to depression but doesn't alter how they look at their lives. The same incident could lead to a spiritual awakening for another person due to the loss of identity experienced as a result of losing their job.

There were five stages I went through during my spiritual awakening. Naturally, I advanced to the next stage after I had learned the lessons I needed to learn in the current stage. There was no expected timeframe to complete my awakening. In fact, upon reaching the fifth stage, it became clear to me that an awakening lasts a lifetime. In other words, I would constantly need to grow, learn higher truths, shed old skin, and dig deeper within myself. Here is a summary of the five stages:

1. **The initial awakening:** I questioned the ideas and beliefs I had always accepted as truth. My lifestyle and some relationships no longer felt aligned with who I was becoming. I also experienced an internal void, or emptiness, as though something were missing.

2. **The dark night of the soul:** My life went from bad to worse as strong pillars that I had previously relied on (such as my job, family unit, and health) came crashing down. As the name suggests, this felt like the darkest and loneliest moment of my life, which forced me to desire healing and breakthrough.

3. **The truth-seeking:** After reaching rock bottom, I made it my mission to get myself out of the dark hole. However, since my old self had been completely cast away, I went searching for new truths that I could build a new foundation on. During this stage, spiritual, philosophical, scientific, sociological, and psychological knowledge became my fascination. I absorbed a bit of everything before coming to my own conclusions.

4. **Confronting the ego:** The ego is the self-concept you form at a young age as a result of your early childhood experiences. It controls your defense mechanisms and the stories you have created about your life. Your ego can also

be the reason behind your self-sabotage, self-doubt, and fear of failure, success, or change. During my spiritual awakening, I had to confront my ego by challenging my limiting beliefs, irrational fears, and self-destructive behaviors. This process took many years, and sometimes, it is still something I must contend with.

5.   **Awareness:** The final stage of my spiritual awakening was when I gained more clarity about my divine purpose and actively lived a transformed life. This stage continues for the rest of my human life because there is no limit to how deeply I can know myself. As I grow older and gain more life experience, my awareness will expand and ultimately cause me to seek higher truths and continue to challenge my ego.

Finding Your Divine Purpose

One of the gifts of a spiritual awakening is finding your divine purpose. Your purpose has always been a part of you; however, due to your past experiences and conditioning, you were not able to intuitively sense what your purpose is. If you are a sensitive person, you may have picked up on certain tendencies, synchronicities, or patterns in your life that pointed toward your purpose. For instance, you may have noticed that your empathy toward people, sociability, and desire to serve others were all pointing toward your calling as a healer. However, you can only know for sure what your calling is when you shed the old self and embrace the empowered version of yourself.

We can define a Divine purpose as the earthly assignment imprinted in your spiritual DNA. Imagine that before you left the spiritual realm and entered into your physical body, you were given an assignment to accomplish in your limited time here on earth. Your mission in your human life is to "wake up" and remember what your assignment is. Since it was given to you, there is no other person capable of doing the job. This also means that you already have the abilities and qualities to carry out this assignment.

Finding your Divine purpose injects meaning into your life. You finally have a reason to wake up hopeful each morning because every day spent working on your assignment feels gratifying. Your purpose can also help you refine your character, filtering out habits, beliefs, and lifestyle choices that aren't aligned with where you are heading. Don't be surprised if you start to feel disconnected from certain people, places, or interests when you find your purpose. Naturally, you will need to sacrifice aspects of who you were and how you lived in order to embrace the new beginning laid out in front of you.

Unfortunately, finding your Divine purpose isn't something you can plan for. You remember your purpose spontaneously, similar to how you spontaneously have an "Aha" moment. Even so, there are a few ways of confirming your purpose once you feel as though you have found it:

1. **Your intuition will tell you.** When we say, "You will know when you've found your purpose," we mean that you will intuitively sense when you are called to live a certain way or dedicate your life to a certain cause. You will feel an unshakable fire within you that will cause you to act on your inclinations.

2. **Assess your strengths.** Your talents are the natural abilities you are born with. You were not given these natural abilities by accident. Your talents can serve as clues indicating what your Divine purpose is. They can show you the best ways in which you can be of service to others.

3. **Read your journal.** Another great way to confirm your purpose is by reading your journal entries. You may not realize it, but there are many personal thoughts and feelings that you share in your journal entries. When looking through your journal, look for recurring desires, ideas, or suggestions that you write down. These can serve as clues to finding your purpose.

4. **Reflect on your childhood.** It can also be good to think back on the dreams or qualities you expressed as a child before you lost your innocence. Back then, you had nothing to prove to the world and were more likely to act, think, and feel like your authentic self. You can also try to remember the hobbies, career field, or TV shows that interested you.

5. **Expose yourself to a variety of literature.** The more knowledge you gain about the world and yourself, the easier it is to sense what resonates with you and what doesn't. Make it your mission to read a variety of literature, watch new and interesting videos on YouTube, or follow insightful podcasts. Seek more knowledge in the topics that end up interesting you. As you gain insight, note down what exactly fascinates you about these various topics.

Activity: Journal Prompts to Help You Discover Your Divine Purpose

Journal prompts are questions that help you access deep parts of your mind. As simple as they are, they allow you to answer personal questions about yourself and gain insight into how you think and feel. It's not always easy to intuitively sense what you are talented at or the kind of work you are passionate about. Thus, journal prompts help you zone in on specific aspects of yourself so you can have more "Aha" moments. Here are five journal prompts to get you started:

1. What makes you happy?
2. What is the one quality you love about yourself?
3. If money wasn't a factor, what kind of work would you spend your life doing?
4. Who inspired you as a child, and why?
5. Who inspires you as an adult, and why?

COMMITMENT #5:

Unlock the Vision for Your Life

CHAPTER 9:

Creating Your Vision

When I dare to be powerful, to use my strength in the service of my vision, then it becomes less and less important whether I am afraid.
— Audre Lorde

Throughout the book, we have explored different aspects of yourself that can get in the way of living an empowered and awakened life. We have also discussed various ways to heal the mind, body, and soul, as well as establish a connection with your Higher Power.

All of this information is only useful if you are determined to use it.

This isn't the first time you have heard about the importance of healing and the process of transformation. It also isn't the first time you have attempted to heal and commit to positive change. So, what will be different this time around? How desperate are you to live the life of your dreams?

It's not enough to be aware of what needs to be changed. You must also visualize what you want your future to look like, and be willing to take the necessary steps to manifest your desired reality. I already know you have the inner power to manifest your highest heart's desire—the only person left to believe it is YOU.

Get Clear On What You Want

So, you have decided that you need change and have set goals for the new direction you would like to take in your life. That's all the preparation you need, right?

Well, not quite.

A crucial part of your preparation is getting clear about your goals. By this, I don't mean refining how your goals are written. Getting clear about your goals is about getting to the bottom of what you genuinely desire. Your genuine desires tend to be hidden underneath the expectations that the world, your family, your boss, or your wounded self has set for you. If you were to sit yourself down and reflect on most of your goals, you would find that although they are extraordinary, they don't impact you on a heart level.

In other words, most of the goals you set tend to be "nice things to have or do" but don't have any personal significance to you. Achieving these kinds of goals would certainly put a smile on your face, but wouldn't testify to the existence of a Higher Power or serve as evidence of being guided by a Divine Purpose.

You are probably scratching your head wondering what your goals have to do with your Higher Power. After all, they are your personal goals. However, when you consider *why* you deeply desire certain things, you can't help but connect your desires to your purpose. In essence, your desires are rooted in what makes you feel alive and brings joy to your life. If your goals aren't having this effect on you, then you may need to clarify them a bit more, until they mirror your purpose.

When your goals mirror your purpose, you won't go back and forth in your mind, wondering whether or not you should take the leap of faith. You won't feel any hesitancy when it comes to doing what it takes to accomplish your goals either. The inner fire activated by your desire, and connected to your heart, will give you enough of a push to take action and make the necessary sacrifices.

Create a Lifestyle Plan for the Key Areas of Your Life

When you are clear on what you want, creating a lifestyle plan will be a straightforward process. Without a plan, your goals remain as wishes. To manifest the lifestyle you desire, you will need to make plans for it, and leave nothing to chance.

A lifestyle plan is a strategy you put in place to materialize goals in several aspects of your life, namely:

- Health and well-being
- Money and finances
- Romantic relationships
- Family
- Friends

- Home environment
- Business and career
- Life purpose

You may place more emphasis on some areas and less emphasis on others, depending on where you are in your life and what you currently desire for yourself. Creating a plan for what you desire to achieve in these areas will give you clarity on what you need to do, how much time or money you need to invest, and the mindset you need to adopt. Having a plan for these various areas of your life will also help you reduce the anxiety that often comes when implementing change, making it easier to commit to your tasks.

Here are seven steps to follow when creating your lifestyle plan:

1. Identify and Eliminate Things You Have Outgrown

Part of the cost of manifesting your ideal lifestyle is the willingness to make sacrifices. There will be some sacrifices that are easy to make and others that aren't. Giving up comforts that have been an integral part of your life for so many years is difficult. However, if these comforts don't reflect the healed and empowered version of yourself, you would do yourself a disservice by keeping them. Acknowledge that your needs have changed and part of self-care is learning how to respond to your new needs.

2. Take a Glimpse Into the Future

Before you write down your plan, you need to journey into the future and envision living as your most authentic self. It's important to mentally see where you are heading so that you understand the amount of effort and *intentionality* you will need to invest into manifesting your dream life.

3. Create Your Lifestyle Plan

Your lifestyle plan should be what bridges the gap between who you are now and who you desire to be. To make crafting your plan easier, you can work backwards. Starting from your desired outcome, work backwards and think about each step you will need to take to achieve those results. Focus on creating small and manageable steps that you can start working on immediately. You can even divide your steps into daily, weekly, and monthly tasks that you can review on a quarterly basis. Lastly, keep your steps specific to the outcomes you desire to achieve. For example, if part of your plan is to improve your health, setting a goal to exercise for 15 minutes three times a week is specific and targeted to your desired outcome.

4. Find Ways to Keep Yourself Accountable

Once you have created your plan, you will need to create structures that keep you accountable for it. Is there a daily planner that you could use to remind you of the tasks you need to complete each day? Do you have access to a mentor or coach who can regularly check on your progress? The more structures you put in place to hold you to your word or ensure that you adhere to your plan, the better!

5. Review Your Progress Regularly

The best way to know if you are moving in the right direction is to have regular check-ins with yourself where you review your progress. Be honest about what you find challenging to complete, what you are enjoying, and the changes you need to make to remain consistent in implementing your plan. It's important to also be upfront about what you need to improve in certain areas. For example, if part of your lifestyle plan is to land a managerial position at work, you will need to upskill yourself and obtain the necessary qualifications to be considered for the role. During your reviews, you can also adjust your time frames to give yourself enough time to gain the experience, knowledge, or funding that you need.

Activity: Visualize Your Dream Day

Set aside 15 minutes in the morning to visualize your dream day. Imagine that you were waking up, some time in the future, to the reality you dream about. The first time you rehearse your dream day, make sure you play it in slow motion. Take your time going through the process of the kind of person you are waking up next to, what your morning routine looks like, where you live and how your home is designed, how you spend your day, and so on. Experience the sense of peace and joy that fills your heart. Picture yourself repeating in your mind, "I have made it!"

Once you have gone through your dream day once in slow motion, start from the beginning and this time increase the speed at which your day plays out. Repeat this visualization until your dream day is playing as fast as possible. Thereafter, pull up a blank screen in your mind and think of a word to describe your dream day. Imagine this word coming up on the blank screen. Look at this word for as long as you desire, then when you are ready, open your eyes. Each time you practice this visualization, ensure that you choose a different word. Now you can spend the rest of the day thinking about the word that describes your dream day.

Conclusion

I n moments where I have felt discouraged, I have often turned to poetry to console my weary soul. Author and spiritual leader, Marianne Williamson, has been an inspiration to me when I think about the journey an awakened woman must travel. In her poem, *Our Deepest Fear*, she speaks of the most common barrier to personal transformation—our own insecurities. Here is an excerpt (Williamson, 1992):

> *We ask ourselves*
> *Who am I to be brilliant, gorgeous, talented, fabulous?*
> *Actually, who are you not to be?*
> *You are a child of God.*
>
> *Your playing small*
> *Does not serve the world.*
> *There's nothing enlightened about shrinking*
> *So that other people won't feel insecure around you.*

There isn't a better piece of writing that describes some of the obstacles I have come across in my life, yet despite having experienced low self-worth and doubted my own glory, I am thankful for having gone through the tough times.

When I choose to think of my life story, I never choose to define myself by the negative experiences I have faced. Yes, it was real and painful, but I have since moved on from there. Like the mythical phoenix that dies and is reborn out of the cloud of smoke and ashes, the challenges I have encountered in my life have been gateways for rebirth and re-emerging as a more resilient version of myself.

We have reached the end of the book and I would like to commend you for making it this far. Together, we have delved into topics that weren't easy to speak about and revisited old memories that we had buried deep in our minds. All of this was done with a single intention—to emphasize the importance of the five commitments you need to make to live an empowered and awakened life.

These commitments were:

1. **Identify and transform self-doubt:** Confronting your limiting beliefs and the perception you have about yourself in relation to others, or in your ability to achieve your goals.

2. **Prioritize your self-care:** Making it a habit to nurture your mental, emotional, and spiritual well-being so you can live a balanced lifestyle.

3. **Develop self-awareness:** Observing your life experiences objectively to identify thought patterns, emotional triggers, and behaviors that aren't enhancing your quality of life.

4. **Connect to your inner wisdom:** Shutting out the world around you and focusing on your inner self so you can quieten your mind and connect to life force energy (the energy of the Divine).

5. **Unlock the vision for your life:** Being clear about what you want and being able to create a comprehensive

plan so you can take action and receive the breakthrough you desire!

With the wealth of knowledge you have learned from this book, I am confident that you are prepared for your transformational journey. Trust in the process and encourage yourself to continue ascending to greater heights and depths of healing, growth, and purpose.

If you have found this book valuable, please leave a review.

References

Boyd, K. (2022, February 1). *50 Inspiring quotes from famous black women to celebrate black history month*. Cafemom.com. https://cafemom.com/entertainment/josh-duggar-new-trial-request-sentencing

Brown, C. (2019, March 21). *25 Inspiring quotes by strong black women*. Medium. https://medium.com/@ghostwriter.cheryl/25-inspiring-quotes-by-strong-black-women-8fd48819f244

Cambridge Dictionary. (2019, November 4). *Enemy meaning in the Cambridge English Dictionary*. Cambridge.org. https://dictionary.cambridge.org/dictionary/english/enemy

Clements, A. (2018, February 21). *Are you low maintenance or do you just have low standards?* Bolde. https://www.bolde.com/low-maintenance-just-low-standards/

Cuncic, A. (2020, June 29). *How to change your negative thought patterns when you have SAD*. Verywell Mind. https://www.verywellmind.com/how-to-change-negative-thinking-3024843

Daniel, T. (2017, April 10). *Getting clear on what you want. How one simple idea took me from confusion to clarity*. Possibility Change. https://possibilitychange.com/confusion-what-you-want/#:~:text=Don

Eatough, E. (2021, November 5). *Out-of-sorts? Strengthening your mind, body, soul connection can help.* Www.betterup.com. https://www.betterup.com/blog/mind-body-and-soul

Esther. (2021, August 12). *How to find your Divine purpose (and fulfill it).* Through the Phases. https://www.throughthephases.com/how-to-find-your-divine-purpose/

Famous Quotes and Sayings. (n.d.). *Top 10 rewire your brain quotes and sayings.* Quotessayings.net. https://quotessayings.net/topics/rewire-your-brain/

Fuller, K. (2021, February 21). *How clutter affects our mental health.* Verywell Mind. https://www.verywellmind.com/decluttering-our-house-to-cleanse-our-minds-5101511

Good Read. (n.d.). *Rick Warren quote.* Www.goodreads.com. https://www.goodreads.com/author/show/711.Rick_Warren

Good Reads. (n.d.-a). *Boundaries quotes (426 quotes).* Www.goodreads.com. https://www.goodreads.com/quotes/tag/boundaries

Good Reads. (n.d.-b). *C.G. Jung quote.* Www.goodreads.com. https://www.goodreads.com/author/show/38285.C_G_Jung

Good Reads. (n.d.-c). *George R.R. Martin quote.* Www.goodreads.com. https://www.goodreads.com/author/show/346732.George_R_R_Martin

Good Reads. (n.d.-d). *J.D. Stroube quote.* Www.goodreads.com. https://www.goodreads.com/author/show/4846190.J_D_Stroube

Good Reads. (n.d.-e). *Self care quotes (591 quotes)*. Www.goodreads. com. https://www.goodreads.com/quotes/tag/self-care

Good Reads. (n.d.-f). *Vision quotes (1856 quotes)*. Www.goodreads. com. https://www.goodreads.com/quotes/tag/vision

Good Reads. (2012). *Maddy Malhotra quote*. Good Reads. https://www.goodreads.com/author/show/7242192. Maddy_Malhotra

Jones, S. (n.d.). *10 Main symptoms of mind clutter*. Learn-fromblogs.com. https://learnfromblogs.com/symptoms-of-mind-clutter

K-Love Fan Awards. (2017, June 1). *Alone with God: How to enjoy His presence*. K-LOVE Fan Awards. https://www.fanawards.com/alone-with-god-enjoy-presence

Kumar, S. (2020, September 14). *How does social environment impacts child's behavior?* Times of India Blog. https://timesofindia.indiatimes.com/readersblog/sawan/how-does-social-environment-impacts-childs-behavior-26029/

McLeod, N. S. (2021, March 22). *80 Black women quotes on self-love, life, and success*. Everyday Power. https://everyday-power.com/black-women-quotes/

Modern Therapy. (2021, March 15). *Self-apologies: How to heal shame and guilt through self-forgiveness*. Modern Therapy. https://moderntherapy.online/blog-2/2021/3/15/self-apologies-how-to-heal-shame-amp-guilt-through-self-forgiveness

Norris, R. (2021, January 14). *9 Ways to set boundaries with your family without getting into a full-blown argument.* Hello Giggles. https://hellogiggles.com/love-sex/family/how-to-set-boundaries-with-family/

Northrup, C. (2020, May 12). *Women's bodies, women's wisdom: Creating physical and emotional health and healing (Newly updated and revised 5th Edition).* Amazon.com. https://www.amazon.com/Womens-Bodies-Wisdom-Creating-Emotional/dp/0525486119

Queen Mary, University of London. (n.d.). *Solitude, spirituality and inner presence.* Solitudes: Past and Present. https://solitudes.qmul.ac.uk/research/solitude-spirituality-and-inner-presence/

Radin, S. (2019, November 13). *How to create boundaries with a toxic family member.* Allure. https://www.allure.com/story/toxic-family-how-create-boundaries

Regan, S. (2021, February 5). *21 Signs you're going through a spiritual awakening and how to embrace it.* Mindbodygreen. https://www.mindbodygreen.com/articles/spiritual-awakening

Ruse, S. (2021, February 11). *The power of self-forgiveness in healing trauma and dissociation.* Stacy Ruse. https://stacyrusecounseling.com/self-forgiveness-trauma-dissociation/

Sadarangani, P. (2020, March 19). *7 Powerful poems to inspire resilience by women poets*. Hive Life Magazine. https://hivelife.com/inspiring-poems-women/

says, H. Y. H. Y. L. 5 W. to D. H. S.-E. (2014, April 16). *3 Types of mental clutter and how to eliminate them*. The Stone Foundation. https://thestonefoundation.com/3-types-of-mental-clutter-and-how-to-eliminate-them/

Scott, E. (2019). *How to make a plan for lasting life changes*. Verywell Mind. https://www.verywellmind.com/how-to-make-a-life-plan-first-steps-3144639

Scott, E. (2021, December 4). *5 Effective ways to clear your mind and reduce stress*. Verywell Mind. https://www.verywellmind.com/how-can-i-clear-my-mind-3144602

Scott, S. (2019, January 12). *How to be more self aware: 8 Tips to boost self-awareness*. Develop Good Habits. https://www.developgoodhabits.com/what-is-self-awareness/

Shine. (2021, February 21). *13 Powerful quotes from black women about self-love*. Shine. https://advice.theshineapp.com/articles/quotes-from-powerful-black-women-all-about-self-love/

Sicinski, A. (2018, April 5). *Here's why raising your standards is the key to goal achievement*. IQ Matrix Blog. https://blog.iqmatrix.com/raising-standards#:~:text=With%20a%20higher%20set%20of

Smith, M., Segal, J., & Robinson, L. (2021, November). *Burnout prevention and treatment*. HelpGuide.org. https://

www.helpguide.org/articles/stress/burnout-preven-tion-and-recovery.htm

Tomm, S. (2018, December 7). *Five reasons the body needs energy.* Sfgate.com. https://healthyeating.sfgate.com/five-reasons-body-needs-energy-4673.html

Van Schneider, T. (2017, June 22). *If you want it, you might get it. The Reticular Activating System explained.* Medium; Desk of van Schneider. https://medium.com/desk-of-van-schneider/if-you-want-it-you-might-get-it-the-reticular-activating-system-explained-761b6ac14e53

Williams, L. (2018, January 30). *I don't know who I am anymore: Grief and loss of identity.* What's Your Grief. https://whatsyourgrief.com/dont-know-anymore-grief-loss-identity/

Williamson, M. (1992). *Our Greatest Fear – Marianne Williamson.* Explorersfoundation.org. https://explorersfoundation.org/glyphery/122.html

About the Author

Mariah Giscombe is a certified Life & Success Coach, NLP Practitioner, and Business Strategist who specializes in helping mission-driven women to breakthrough self-doubt and get clarity in their lives so that they stop wasting time on things that are blocking their success and keeping them stuck.

Her signature approach combines life coaching, business strategy, and Neuro Linguistic mindset techniques that guides women to incorporate ease, flow and inner strength into their lives by shifting their mindset and becoming deliberate, not desperate, creators.

She has a specialized honours degree in Sociology from York University, postgraduate studies in Strategic Business Management, and is 2015 Black Canadian Awards Community Role Model Honouree.

Mariah lives in Toronto, Canada and regularly teaches workshops and gives talks as an expert in personal development and empowerment, helping women to confidently take their lives to the next level.

Meet Mariah and learn more at

www.mariahgiscombe.com

CPSIA information can be obtained
at www.ICGtesting.com
Printed in the USA
LVHW110016150822
725927LV00004B/437